Andrew Jack & Jenny

Royal Navy Nicknames
Origins & History
Paul White

PAUL WHITE

Copyright © Paul White 2018

TOAD Publishing

All rights reserved. This book or any portion thereof

may not be reproduced or used in any manner whatsoever

without the express written permission of the publisher

except for the use of brief quotations in a book review.

pwauthor@mail.com

DEDICATION

Many books of quotations include a caustic quote (*wrongly*) attributed to Sir Winston Churchill.

The earliest source commonly cited for this quip is the diary of former British diplomat, politician and author, Harold Nicolson, in a diary entry dated August 17, 1950.

The story goes something like this...

When Winston was at the Admiralty, the Board objected to a suggestion of his, on the grounds it would not be in accord with naval tradition.

"Naval tradition? Naval tradition?" said Winston. "Monstrous. Nothing but rum, sodomy, prayers and the lash."

(*Sometimes reported as "rum, buggery and the lash," using the old British slang term "buggery" to refer to homosexual acts.*)

When later asked by Montague-Browne, Churchills most respected biographer, Churchill responded: "I never said it. I wish I had."

It seems this miss quote has some comparison with naval phrases dating from the 19th century "Ashore, it's wine, women and song, aboard it is rum, bum and concertina."

According to a 20th-century Canadian merchant seaman of the early '1940s (*via GB*)

"When you went ashore, there was the rum, bum and the 'baccy girl'. She was there for that purpose; she knew what her job was, she knew it well."

The word 'baccy' in this instant has little to do with tobacco but is a derivative of 'Bacchante' the ancient Greek word for a female (drunken) reveller. After Bacchus, the Greek god of wine.

I'll leave you to draw your own conclusions from therein.

Therefore, the dedication for this book, The Andrew, Jack & Jenny, must be,

"To all the Baccy girls, in all the ports, in all the world."

I know Jack would like it to be so.

THE ANDREW, JACK & JENNY

Table of Content

Dedication - Page Three

Forward - Page Seven

Etymology - Page Eleven

Taxonomy - Page Thirteen

Elucidation

The Andrew - Page Twenty One

Jack - Page Twenty Three

Jenny - Page Twenty Nine

Glossary

Alphabetical - Page Thirty Three

Odds & Sods - Page Three Seven Nine

Jenny's Names - Page Three Eight Five

Afterword - Page Three Nine One

About the Author - Page Three Nine Three

PAUL WHITE

FORWARD
(For'ard)

Unlike the civilian nicknames we get labelled with; those our classmates called us at school, the one's various work colleagues may apply to us from time to time, or the ones our siblings find amusing, a military nickname has greater significance, it holds a value only fully comprehended by our contemporaries.

Arguably, the Royal Navy has the most entrenched tradition among the services for bestowing nicknames, names not only for each sailor but for places, equipment and actions.

This book, The Andrew, Jack & Jenny, focuses primarily on the names given to each skin and essence the moment they became a matelot.

Royal Naval nicknames are not chosen by the recipient, they are bestowed, irrevocably, by custom and tradition. Yet, each sailor soon becomes attached to their 'new' name, which grows into a large part of their identity, even influencing their character.

It soon becomes the name which is spoken with pride in answer to the question "Who are you?"

How these names, these nom de plumes came to be and where they originated is frequently lost in the grey sea-mist of passing time. Especially as new generations of Jolly Jack Tars bequeath new versions and modern interpretations of older, vintage, even historic monikers.

However, some nicknames are so entrenched in history it is doubtful they shall ever alter. These are those which reflect great heroes and remarkable men and women – pirates, explorers, admirals, inventors, navigators. These include people such as Doctor Livingstone, but also lesser-known figures such as Admiral Lord Charlie Beresford.

On the other hand, there are those which only lend their names for a generation or two, the successful sportsmen and women, music hall acts and stars of the silver screen along with popular television personalities; all characters Jack refers to in pursuit of original nickname creation. These, often relatively short-lived, 'celebrity names', are one reason for finding the origin and history behind many nicknames a daunting and often impossible task.

Many navy nicknames have an origin and a history from way beyond these shores. Jack was never one to dismiss opportunity of originality and absorbed foreign words, ideas and ideologies, altering the pronunciation and spelling to suit; hence melding them into the uniqueness of Royal Naval Jackspeak.

Here, in 'The Andrew, Jack & Jenny,' I have researched the darkest bilges of doubt and plumbed the deepest oceans of uncertainty to find the genuine and most academically accepted answers to the origins and history of these Royal Navy Nicknames.

The result is a book with many factual acknowledgements, recognised accuracy and detail... along with much speculation, conjecture, theories and hearsay, possibly as many as there were before my research began. Such is the complexity of the search for undeniable proof.

This has led to a comprehensive collection of Royal Navy Nicknames which are listed alphabetically.

Those individual names, the ones which are so random, capricious and arbitrary they defy categorisation, follow the main indexation, as do those relating to Jenny Wrens alone.

Despite, or it may be in-spite, of all the above, I have begun this book with a section given over to the understanding of the various forms of nicknames such as 'personality', 'incident' and 'characteristics', the explanation of the term 'nickname' and that of 'The Andrew', 'Jack' & 'Jenny', along with as much detail on the origination of each given name and all relevant historical significance pertinent.

It is all carefully logged here as a recording of Royal Naval social history, as a legacy for future generations.

To ensure this book's historical authenticity it includes many traditional terminology and figures of speech used in the respective eras.

Some may find certain expressions and terms undesirable or offensive when measured against today's accepted social standards. Therefore, readers discretion is advised.

ETYMOLOGY

MIDDLE ENGLISH	*AN EKE-NAME*
MIDDLE ENGLISH	*EKE (ADDITION)*
ENGLISH	*EKE*
ENGLISH	*A NEKE NAME*
LATE MIDDLE ENGLISH	*NICKNAME*

The compound word ekename, literally meaning 'additional name', was attested as early as 1303.

This word was derived from the Old English phrase *eaca,* 'an increase', related to eacian, 'to increase'.

By the fifteenth century, the misdivision of the syllables of the phrase 'an ekename' led to its rephrasing as 'a nekename'.

Though the spelling has changed, the pronunciation and meaning of the word have remained relatively stable since.

'A nickname' is a substitute for the proper name of a familiar person, place, or thing, for affection or ridicule.

The term *hypocoristic* is used to refer to a nickname of affection between those in love or with a close emotional bond, compared with a term of endearment.

The term *diminutive* name refers to nicknames that convey smallness, hence something regarded with affection or familiarity (*e.g. referring to children*), or contempt.

The distinction between the two is often blurred. It is a form of endearment and amusement. As a concept, it is distinct from both pseudonym and stage name and from a title, (*for example, City of Fountains*), although there may be overlap in these concepts.

A *moniker* also means a nickname or personal name.

The word often distinguishes personal names from nicknames that became proper names out of former nicknames. English examples are Bob and Rob, nickname variants for Robert.

A nickname is often considered desirable, symbolising a form of acceptance, but can sometimes be a form of ridicule.

Taxonomy

This section is for explanation and clarification for derivatives of nicknaming.

This information is general, NOT Royal Navy specific.

In 'The Andrew, Jack & Jenny', *Short names*, *Cognomens*, *Hypocorisms* and *Diminutives* are all classed as nicknames.

Nicknames may refer to a person's occupation, social standing or title.

They may also refer to characteristics of a person or take into consideration their past actions.

Occupational.

Names could be, Bones, Sawbones, Doc or Scab lifter, for a forensic scientist, surgeon, or mortician

Sparky and Greenie works for an electrician and/or radio operator.

Geek, Nerd etc. for a computer technician or programmer.

Physical.

Beanpole, Streaka (piss), Lanky for a person who is tall. Shorty, short-arse or Midge for a short person. Or vice-versa in the negative.

Red, Ginge, Rusty for a person with red hair, while Blondie is associated with a blonde-haired female.

Curly for a person without hair, as in "Curley" from "The Three Stooges". Bald men are often referred to as Chromedome.

Sometimes nicknames are based on things that are not a part of a person's body but alter a person's physical appearance.

Speccy four-eyes for a person with glasses. Metal mouth or Braceface for a person with braces.

Personality.

Motormouth and Chatterbox if they won't shut up.

A pessimist may be called Sad Sack, or Debbie Downer

Strong-willed Thatcher was known as The Iron Lady.

Mental.

Einstein, referring to the famous physicist.

Sherlock, in reference to A. C. Doyle's Sherlock Holmes.

Brainiac, as in the fictional DC Comics character.

Dopey, as in the dwarf who doesn't speak, from Snow White

Lifestyle.

Hot Lips is the character Margaret Houlihan in the TV series M*A*S*H.

Mary Mallon (1870–1938) was nicknamed Typhoid Mary.

Abbreviation or modification

Margaret contracts to Greta.

DJ works for Daniel James

Fanny from Frances, Walt from Walter.

Phonetic.

Len from Leonard.

Letter swapping.

During the middle ages, the letter R would often be swapped for either L or D, hence Hal from Harry, Molly from Mary, Sadie from Sarah, from Robert, Rob, Bob. Richard begat Rick, Dick, and Bill for Will.

Name portions.

Sometimes a nickname can come from the beginning of a given name: Chris from Christopher/Christina; Ed from Edward, Edmond, Edgar.

End of name: Drew from Andrew, Beth from Elizabeth, Bel, Bell, Bella or Belle from Isabelle/Isabella

Middle of name: Liz from Elizabeth, Tori from Victoria or Del or Della from Adelaide.

Addition of diminutives.

Before the 17th century, most nicknames had the diminutive ending 'in' or 'kin'.

where the ending was attached to the first syllable: Watkin for Walter via Wat-kin; Hobkin from Robert via Hob-kin; or Thompkin from Thomas via Thom-Kin. While most of these have died away, a few remain, such as Robin (Rob-in, from Robert), Hank (Hen-Kin from Henry), Jack (Jan-kin from John), and Colin (Col-in from Nicolas).

Many nicknames drop the final one or two letters and add ether ie/ee/y as a diminutive ending: Davy from David, Charlie from Charles, Mikey from Michael, Jimmy from James and Marty from Martin.

Initialization.

Which forms a nickname from a person's initials: A.C. Slater from Albert Clifford Slater, or Dubya for George W. Bush, a Texan pronunciation of the name of the letter 'W', President Bush's middle initial.

Attached suffix.

Gazza for footballer Paul Gascoigne (though used more widely in Australia for Gary) and similar "zza" forms Prezza, as in John Prescot the Yorkshire politician. Others use the Oxford 'er'.

Second name.

Use variations of a person's first and middle name. For example, a person may have the name Mary Elizabeth but has the nickname "Maz" or "Miz" by combining Mary and Liz.

Surname. This is the primary category for generating Royal Navy nicknames. (although not exclusively).

Nobby for Clark or Clarke, Dusty for Miller, Chalky for White, Bunny for Reed, Yosser for Hughes.

The RN uses several variations of these more common examples.

Common prefixes.

Mac for someone with the name Macmillan, McIntyre, McCarthy etc.

Fitz for someone with the name Fitzgerald, Fitzpatrick is common.

Variations on the surname.

Brownie for someone with the name Brown

Jeff for someone with the name Geoffrey, Jeffry, Jeffreys, etc.

Smittie (or Smitty) for someone with the name Smith, Smythe, Goldsmith, etc.

Action/incident

A specific incident or action can sometimes generate a nickname.

Capability Brown, the famous landscape gardener acquired his nickname because he frequently told his clients the landscape was "capable of improvement".

Thirteen for Dr Remy Hadley from TV's House M.D., because she was assigned the number 13 in her job interview process and continued to be called by her number even after she was hired.

Notable/fictional character.

Napoleon or Hitler ("he is a little Hitler"), for someone with a dictatorial manner.

Pollyanna for someone with a very optimistic view of things.

Hawkeye from the novel The Last of the Mohicans; as in 'Hawkeye' Pierce, from M*A*S*H.

Place of origin/residence.

Sometimes, a nickname may be related to their place of origin or residence.

Janner for a Cornishman, Scouse from Liverpool or Geordie, the Newcastle lad.

Reputation.

John Wayne was known as The Duke. The Angel of Death was Josef Mengele.

The list of possibilities is almost endless.

I have built a comprehensive list of Royal Naval nicknames, most are based on at least one of the above categories, but some are so random, capricious and arbitrary they defy categorisation. They follow the main indexation, as do those relating to Jenny Wrens, along with some additional information.

Elucidation

The Andrew

THE ANDREW is the traditional lower-deck colloquial term for the Royal Navy.

The common theory being the Royal Navy is nicknamed after Lieutenant Andrew Miller, a much-feared press gang operator in the Portsmouth area during the Napoleonic wars. So successful was Andrew Miller, it was said he *"owned the Royal Navy."*

However, no documentary evidence of his existence has yet been found.

Press gangs were a form of recruitment when ships were short of crew. A small band of sailors led by an officer would seize men for military service. There were some exemptions, but often these were ignored.

The press gang was last officially used during the Napoleonic Wars between 1803-1815.

The need for impressment died out in the 1850s when continuous service was introduced for sailors wanting to make the navy their career.

However, in the twentieth century another type of impressment, called national service, was used until the 1960s.

However, the right to use impressment was retained and is still a legal option to this day.

Another theory for the nickname 'The Andrew' comes from the fact that St Andrew is the patron saint of sailors and fishermen.

As accurate as this suggestion may be, it is too simple, it does not hold the legendary impression or sensationalism of the Andrew Miller legend.

The Royal Navy is also jocularly referred to as the Grey Funnel Line.

Ship owning companies, or lines, paint their steam ship's funnels in distinctive colours, such as Cunard's red and black or the eponymous Blue Funnel Line.

Royal Navy ships funnels are plain grey.

JACK

(*Also, jacktar, jack-tar or tar*)

There is some dispute among historians about the origin of the term JACK, but it was a common generic, frequently used and often employed to refer to the mass of common people.

Both historically and in regional dialects, the names Jack and John were frequently interchanged as were the words 'Jock' and 'Jan' which are other derivations.

What sets sailors apart from that *'mass of common people'* is the addition of the word 'Tar'.

In the age of wooden sailing vessels, a ship's rigging was of hemp rope, which could rot quickly in the wet, salty sea air. To avoid this, the ropes and cables of the standing rig were soaked in tar, which needed to be reapplied at frequent intervals.

At that time sailors, along with much of the civilian population, wore their hair long. Whether this was a fashion or simply for convenience is open to conjecture.

However, aboard ships on the high seas the wind would blow any unfastened long hair, which often became caught in ropes and rigging. To counteract this, sailors would braid their hair and dip it in the pitch (tar) used to seal the decks and waterproof ropes.

These tarred pigtails fell out of fashion around 1825. The last official recorded pigtail worn in the Royal Navy is in 1827.

It is also ventured that clothing was tarred to waterproof them, hence the origin of the name Tarpaulin, the same name given to a sailor's hat in the late 1600's.

The amalgamation of both 'Jack' and 'Tar' soon became a customary and familiar name for Royal Navy sailors.

As the need for using hot pitch on ships became redundant the word 'Tar' faded from general usage.

However, the word 'Jack' remains a popular nickname for matelots to this day.

Another factor to consider is the other use of the word 'Jack' when referring to a flag.

The Union Flag, often referred to as the Union Jack is said to result from the signature *Jacques of King James I* in whose reign (*1603-1625*) the Union Jack was designed.

James VI of Scotland (*Jacques*) inherited the English and Irish thrones in 1603 as James I, thereby uniting the crowns of England, Scotland and Ireland in a personal union. Although the three kingdoms remained separate states.

On 12 April 1606, a new flag to represent the regal union between England and Scotland was specified in a royal decree, according to which the flag of England (*a red cross on a white background, known as St George's Cross*), and the flag of Scotland (*a white saltire on a blue background, known as the Saltire or St Andrew's Cross*), would be joined together, forming the flag of England and Scotland for maritime purposes.

King James also began to refer to a "Kingdom of Great Britaine", although the union remained a personal one.

The present design of the Union Flag dates from a Royal Proclamation following the union of Great Britain and Ireland in 1801. This flag combines red saltire of St Patrick, to represent

Ireland, with the Union of England and Scotland flag to produce the Union Flag we know today.

Notably, Wales is not represented separately in the Union Flag, as the flag was designed after the invasion of Wales in 1282. Hence Wales was classified as a 'home country of England and has no independent representation on the flag.

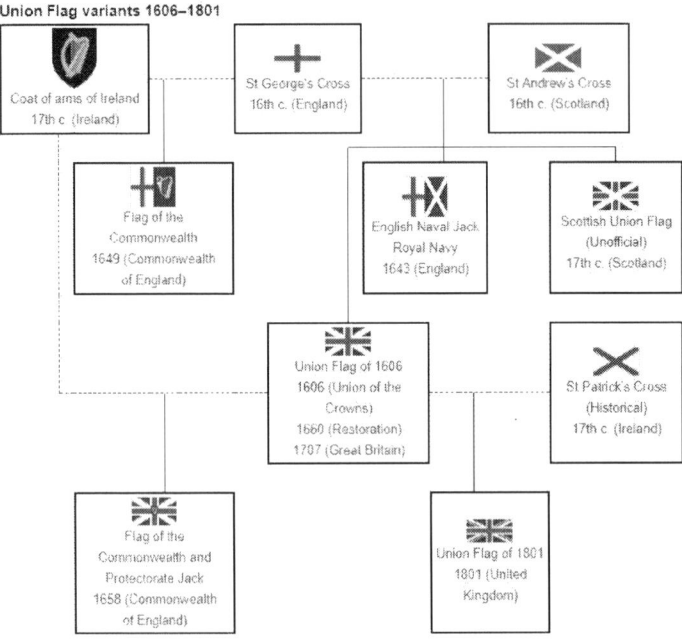

It is often stated the Union Flag should only be described as the Union Jack when flown in the bows of a warship, but this is a relatively recent idea.

From early in its life the Admiralty itself frequently referred to the flag as the Union Jack, whatever its use and in 1902 an Admiralty circular announced *'Their Lordships decision'* that either name could be used officially.

In 1908, a government minister stated, in response to a parliamentary question, that;

"The Union Jack should be regarded as the National flag."

PAUL WHITE

JENNY
(WRNS)

JENNY and JENNY WREN are both the official and the affectionately respected nicknames given to members of the Women's Royal Naval Service.

The Women's Royal Naval Service (WRNS) was founded in November 1917, as a branch of the Royal Navy, during the First World War.

On 10 October 1918, nineteen-year-old Josephine Carr from Cork, became the first Wren to die on active service, when the ship she was travelling on, the RMS Leinster, was torpedoed.

By the end of the war, the WRNS had 5,500 members, 500 of them officers.

In addition, about 2,000 members of the WRAF had previously served with the WRNS supporting the Royal Naval Air Service and were transferred on the creation of the Royal Air Force.

The WRNS disbanded in 1919.

The WRNS was revived in 1939, at the beginning of the Second World War, with an expanded list of allowable activities, including flying transport planes. At its peak, in 1944 it had 75,000 active servicewomen.

During the war, there were 100 deaths. One of the slogans used in recruiting posters was "Join the Wrens - free a man for the fleet."

The WRNS remained in existence after the war and was finally integrated into the regular Royal Navy in 1993 when women could serve on board navy vessels as full members of the crew.

In October 1990, during the Gulf War, HMS Brilliant carried the first women to officially serve on an operational warship. The first woman in the Royal Navy to be awarded the Military Cross was medic Able Seaman Kate Nesbitt, for actions in Afghanistan in 2009.

Before 1993, all women in the Royal Navy were members of the WRNS except nurses, who joined (and still join) Queen Alexandra's Royal Naval Nursing Service.

Medical and dental officers, who were commissioned directly into the Royal Navy, held RN ranks and wore WRNS uniform with gold RN insignia.

Female sailors are still affectionally known by the nicknames "Wrens" or Jennies ("Jenny Wrens") in naval slang, particularly by armed forces veterans.

How long this tradition will continue, or be allowed to continue, is unknown.

PAUL WHITE

Glossary

This following list comprises the most common names found in the Royal Naval archival records of ratings who served circa 1955 to 1985. Whilst this list is extensive, it is practically impossible to be fully comprehensive.

Surnames of British sailors which start 'X' or 'Z' are so rare there are none in this book. Neither, surprisingly, are any surnames beginning with the letter 'I'.

An anomaly I am sure.

Following the main alphabetical listing are two further lists, they comprise some of the more inventive and individual nicknames given to some ratings and some of the monikers associated with WRNS.

This glossary frequently gives one or more spellings for each name. Other, or similar versions, of names may exist.

Many of the accompanying nicknames are often applied to these name variants.

PAUL WHITE

A

ALPHA

ABBOT

Bud *Abbot*

This name is given in relation to William Alexander *'Bud'* Abbott, The American actor who was also a producer and comedian He is probably best remembered for playing the 'straight man' of the comedy duo, **Abbott and Costello.**

Abbott died of cancer, aged 76 in 1974, at his home in Woodland Hills, Los Angeles. His remains were cremated and his ashes scattered onto the Pacific.

ADAIR

Red *Adair*

Paul Neal *'Red'* Adair was the undisputed king of oil well fire-fighting for over 50 years.

Reds rise came during the post-World War II increase in oil and gas drilling and exploration throughout the Middle East.

From fires known as the ***Devil's Cigarette Lighter***, (Sahara Desert in 1962), the ***Piper Alpha platform*** disaster (North Sea 1988), to the torched oil fields of ***post-Gulf-War Kuwait***, Red Adair was at called to every major fire.

Unknown to many, Red supported several charitable organizations, many dedicated to children's health.

After Reds death in 2004, Sunny Adair (*Red's granddaughter and only living relative*), continues this legacy through the **Red Adair Foundation**. The foundations primary beneficiary is the ***Shriners' Children's Hospital*** in Galveston, Texas, which specialises in treating paediatric burn injuries

ADAMS

1, Fanny *Adams*

This is well documented and has a direct connection with RN sailors. Read on and you will understand why.

Fanny Adams, AKA *Sweet Fanny Adams*, was the child victim of Victorian murder Mr Frederick Baker, a solicitor's clerk, who was aged 24 at the time.

Fanny, (Frances Adams), was murdered when she was nine years old. The murder took place in Alton, Hampshire, on 24 April 1867.

As the murder was extraordinarily brutal it caused a national outcry.

Court records and newspaper articles report, Fanny was taken to a hop garden where Frederick Baker chopped her body into small pieces. Some, allegedly, turned up in the ***Royal Navy's Deptford Victualling Yard***.

Other pieces were never found.

Frederick Baker hanged in December 1867, after being tried and found guilty at Winchester.

As it happens... Fanny's murder coincided with the introduction of ***tinned mutton*** into the Royal Navy.

Many matelots suggested these new tinned victuals contained the unfound butchered remains of Fanny Adams.

The mutton was delivered in large tins which were utilised as cooking pots, giving rise to the name 'Fanny' for a large metal cooking vessel.

This all led to 'Fanny Adams' becoming slang for mutton stew, (*later including corned beef, also known as corned dog*).

Latterly, the term 'Fanny' has become used for anything worthless, as in, ***'Sweet Fanny Adams,*** or just ***'Sweet F.A.'*** to mean ***'nothing at all'***.

A modern-day exchangeable euphemism using F.A. is ***'fuck all'***.

Note: *[Corned is an old English word, a name for small chunks of salt (corns), which were used for preserving meat, so Corned Mutton (or Corned Beef), simply means Salted.]*

2, Daisy *Adams.*

I can find no clear-cut facts for the name Daisy to be linked to Adams, beyond the following two possibilities. But if you know otherwise, please inform me.

A,

Daisy *Irene* Adams was the oldest person in the United Kingdom, between the dates of 17 March 1993 and her death on 8 December 1993.

Daisy died aged 113 years, 161 days. She outlived her husband and three of her five children.

Daisy's husband was killed in battle on the first day of the Somme. So, Daisy was widowed when she was in her thirties.

Daisy's son, Ted, put her longevity down to "living a quiet life".

However, as Daisy's notoriety for living a long life did not arise until 1993, it seems she is not the reason for the originality of this word association regarding nicknames. Which leaves...

B,

An American lady called Daisy *Elizabeth* Adams, who was born in Reading, Pennsylvania in or around August the 8th 1883? (*we think*).

Records show Daisy devoted her life to social causes, beginning with issues important to herself as a black housewife.

Actively involved in the suffrage movement, Daisy gave her first women's rights tea in 1912

Was it this Daisy, who was known well enough in the early 19th century, who gave rise for Jack to use her name?

It seems doubtful, but stranger things have happened at sea.

ATKINS

Tommy *Atkins*

There is NO dispute regarding this name as it is well documented.

1794 in Flanders, at the height of the Battle of Boxtel, the Duke of Wellington is with his first command, the 33rd Regiment of Foot. They are engaged in bloody hand-to-hand fighting when the Duke sees a soldier lying mortally wounded in the mud.

(History records him as Private Thomas Atkins.)

> ***"It's all right, sir, all in a day's work"***
>
> the brave soldier says, just before he dies.

...

1815, the 'Iron Duke' is 46 years old. The War Office ask him for a name which could be used as an *'example name'* in a specimen leaflet which instructed the enlisted men how to correctly fill out the newly introduced *'Soldier's Pocket Book'.*

The Duke suggests the example name should be **Private Thomas Atkins, of the British Grenadiers.**

Soldiers pay books thereafter were known as ***'Tommies'*** and, if you were in receipt of one, you were also known as a ***'Tommy'**,* thus giving rise to the nickname for British soldiers.

The name 'Tommy Atkins' was popularised in a Rudyard Kipling poem highlighting the public disdain for British soldiers serving in WW1.

I went into a public 'ouse to get a pint o' beer,

The publican 'e up an' sez, " We serve no red-coats here."

The girls be'ind the bar they laughed an' giggled fit to die,

I outs into the street again an' to myself sez I:

O it's Tommy this, an' Tommy that, an' " Tommy, go away ";

But it's " Thank you, Mister Atkins," when the band begins to play.

The band begins to play, my boys, the band begins to play,

O it's " Thank you, Mister Atkins," when the band begins to play.

I went into a theatre as sober as could be,

They gave a drunk civilian room, but 'adn't none for me;

They sent me to the gallery or round the music-'alls,

But when it comes to fightin', Lord! they'll shove me in the stalls!

For it's Tommy this, an' Tommy that, an' " Tommy, wait outside ";

But it's " Special train for Atkins " when the troopers on the tide.

The troopships on the tide, my boys, the troopships on the tide,

O it's " Special train for Atkins " when the troopers on the tide.

Yes, makin' mock o' uniforms that guard you while you sleep

Is cheaper than them uniforms, an' they're starvation cheap.

An' hustlin' drunken soldiers when they're goin' large a bit

Is five times better business than paradin' in full kit.

Then it's Tommy this, an' Tommy that, an` Tommy, 'ow's yer soul? "

But it's " Thin red line of 'eroes " when the drums begin to roll

The drums begin to roll, my boys, the drums begin to roll,

O it's " Thin red line of 'eroes, " when the drums begin to roll.

We aren't no thin red 'eroes, nor we aren't no blackguards too,

But single men in barricks, most remarkable like you;

An' if sometimes our conduck isn't all your fancy paints,

Why, single men in barricks don't grow into plaster saints;

While it's Tommy this, an' Tommy that, an` Tommy, fall be'ind,"

But it's " Please to walk in front, sir," when there's trouble in the wind

There's trouble in the wind, my boys, there's trouble in the wind,

O it's " Please to walk in front, sir," when there's trouble in the wind.

You talk o' better food for us, an' schools, an' fires, an' all:

We'll wait for extry rations if you treat us rational.

Don't mess about the cook-room slops, but prove it to our face

The Widow's Uniform is not the soldier-man's disgrace.

For it's Tommy this, an' Tommy that, an` Chuck him out, the brute! "

But it's " Saviour of 'is country " when the guns begin to shoot;

An' it's Tommy this, an' Tommy that, an' anything you please;

An 'Tommy ain't a bloomin' fool - you bet that Tommy sees!

ALLEN (ALLAN)

Darby *Allen*

Very little information exists for any conclusion to be drawn about this becoming a 'standard' Naval nickname.

There are two schools of thought, both of which may be wide of the mark.

The first, is the name Allen/Allan is prominent in the history of the city of Derby and therefore it is possible, if several *'Allens'* served at the same time, one or more could be bestowed the name 'Derby'; as 'Scouse' is used for those who hail from Liverpool.

The second thought is the name may be a corruption of the traditional Scottish ballad, **'Barbra Allen'***?*

The earliest texts date from the 18th century, but the song is older. Samuel Pepys recorded hearing it at a social gathering on the 2nd January 1666, according to his diary.

> "… but above all my dear Mrs. Knipp, with whom I sang; and in perfect pleasure, I was to hear her sing and especially her little Scotch song of Barbary Allen."

NOTE: Mrs Knepp an actress, singer, and dancer of the King's Company features regularly in Pepys' diary.

He nicknamed her **'Bab Allen'**.

Twas in the merry month of May
When green buds all were swelling,
Sweet William on his deathbed lay
For love of Barbara Allen.

He sent his servant to the town
To the place where she was dwelling,
Saying you must come, to my master dear
If your name be Barbara Allen.

So slowly, slowly she got up
And slowly she drew nigh him,
And the only words to him did say
Young man, I think you're dying.

He turned his face unto the wall
And death was in him welling,

Good-bye, good-bye, to my friends all
Be good to Barbara Allen.

When he was dead and laid in grave
She heard the death bells knelling
And every stroke to her did say
Hard-hearted Barbara Allen.

Oh mother, oh mother go dig my grave
Make it both long and narrow,
Since my love died for me to-day,
I'll die for him tomorrow.'

'Darbies' are also a slang name for handcuffs, but once again no direct association can be testified.

(*Although some may disagree* !)

ALLCOCK

I shall leave you to your own devices when considering this name. I am sure you will have served with at least on Allcock?

ALMOND

Nutty *Almond*

Referring to the seed of a tree and, to the fact, all sweet and snacks are known as 'Nutty'.

AUSTIN/AUSTEN

Bunny *Austin*

Jack was never one to worry about '*borrowing*' names from prominent people of the time; this one is taken from Henry Wilfred *'Bunny'* Austin, an English tennis player.

Bunny lived a life of glamour and celebrity status. He was an early, if not the original 'playboy'.

He was the first player to wear tennis shorts on Centre Court at Wimbledon. (1932).

Bunny married an actress, played tennis with Charlie Chaplin, knew Queen Mary and President Franklin Delano Roosevelt. He even designed his own tennis racquets.

He was the last British player to reach the men's singles finals at Wimbledon, (*until Andy Murray in 2012.*)

Austin's nickname (Bunny), was taken from a character in the comic strip, *"Pip, Squeak and Wilfred",* forever associating the name Bunny and Austin, at least in Jack's mind.

PAUL WHITE

B
Bravo

BACON

1, Crispy (streaky) Bacon

2, Piggy *Bacon*

3, Kevin *Bacon* (*modern*)

Kevin (*Norwood*) Bacon is an American actor and musician.

He starred in the films Footloose, JFK, A Few Good Men, Apollo 13, and Mystic River and is known for taking on dark roles, like the sadistic guard in Sleepers and the child abuser in The Woodsman.

He has recently, (*2017/18*), become an icon for the concept of interconnectedness (*as in social networks*), which was popularised in the game "Six Degrees of Kevin Bacon" and with TV 'phone commercials.

Kevin created SixDegrees.org, a charitable foundation following its success.

BAILEY (Baily/Baley)

1, Bill *Bailey*

Taken from *'Bill Bailey, Won't You Please Come Home?'* a song from the early 1900's

The words and music are written by Hughie Cannon an American songwriter.

2, Beetles *Bailey*

Beetle Bailey was an American comic strip by cartoonist Mort Walker. Beetle is set in a fictional USA military post.

The cartoon first appeared in September 1950 and continued for over 67 years.

Mort is quoted, *"If you want to truly know me, read my comic strip every day."*

He created 24,562 Beetle Bailey strips. Which it is said contained his personal philosophy of life.

He died on January 27th, 2018.

3, Pearl *Bailey*

Pearl Mae Bailey, first appeared in vaudeville. In 1946 she debuted on Broadway in 'St Louis Woman'.

Pearl won a Tony Award for the title role of 'Hello, Dolly!' in 1968. (An all-black cast.)

"Takes Two to Tango" was Pearls top ten hit 1952. She received a Screen Actors Guild Life Achievement Award in 1976 and the Presidential Medal of Freedom on October 17, 1988.

4, It is also possible 'Pearl' is simply a play on words from *'Pearl Barley'* a cook's ingredient.

5, Buster *Bailey*

As many Jazz musicians from Memphis, Buster Bailey started his career by playing with W.C. Handy's Orchestra.

Bailey's smooth, often fast clarinet style made him a sought-after session musician.

During the 1950 & 60's Buster played with Henry "Red" Allen and many others. In 1965 he joined Louis Armstong and his All-Stars and continued to play with them until he died in 1967.

BAKER

1, Ma *Baker*

The name is taken from a woman called Kate Barker, better known to many as Ma Barker, (sometimes as Arizona Barker).

The band 'Boney M' changed the spelling for their 1977 hit song 'Ma Baker', *"Because they felt it sounded better."*

Kate Barker, mother of several sons who became the 'Barker gang' during the *'public enemy era,'* in the American Midwest

Barker was killed during a shoot-out with the FBI, which sealed her notoriety as a ruthless crime matriarch who controlled and organized her sons' crimes.

J. Edgar Hoover described her as,

"the most vicious, dangerous and resourceful criminal brain of the last decade".

2, Dogs *Baker*

No need to call the RSPCA, the name does not refer to our furry friends.

Dogs seems to be a corruption of the word 'Doughy', a name often given to a Baker.

3, Bagsy *Baker*

An English slang term (from 1866), quite simply, the vernacular for the word 'bag'.

Etymologically it is related to the way small-game hunters stored kill in bags.

It is suggested this came about when hunting,

To lay claim to a kill, shooters would 'Bagsy' it, by saying so as they quickly stuffed the game into their own bag.

How this name became associated with a person called Baker, or how it entered the Naval vernacular is not recorded.

BANKS

Gordon *Banks*

Taken by Jack from this popular Leicester and England goalkeeper from the 1960's & 70's

Gordon Banks, OBE, made 628 appearances during his 15-year career in Football.

He won 73 caps and is regarded as one of the all-time great goalkeepers.

He was named FWA Footballer of the Year in 1972 and FIFA Goalkeeper of the Year on six occasions.

BANNISTER

1, Roger *Bannister*

Not difficult to understand Jack taking a liking to this man's name.

Sir Roger Gilbert Bannister, a middle-distance athlete, physician and academic, was the first person to run a sub-four-minute mile

He achieved this feat on 6 May 1954 at Iffley Road track, in Oxford. Chris Chataway and Chris Brasher were his pacemakers.

The time recorded was 3 minutes 59.4 seconds. Bannister's record only lasted 46 days.

He became a distinguished neurologist and Master of Pembroke College, Oxford.

Once asked if running the sub-4-minute mile was his proudest achievement, he said he was prouder of his contribution to academic medicine into the responses of the nervous system.

Bannister was patron of the MSA Trust.

He was diagnosed with Parkinson's disease in 2011

2, Minnie *Bannister*

Jack has always enjoyed a good laugh. Using this name confirms that.

Henry Crun and Minnie Bannister are two characters from the 1950s radio comedy 'The Goon Show'. They were performed by Peter Sellers and Spike Milligan respectively.

They are elderly characters in many sketches, often in occupations to which they are ill-suited. Such as members of a lifeboat crew or the East Acton Volunteer Auxiliary Civilian Fire Brigade.

Minnie's catchphrase was *"we'll all be murdered in our beds"*.

The characters have several ways of taking their time to answer the front door. In one such sketch, Minnie is walking down several flights of stairs. After about a minute worth of listening to her footsteps, Henry says, *"I can't understand it, we live in a bungalow!"*

Clearly, the humour and the popularity of the 'Goon Show' caused many a poor matelot to be christened 'Minnie'.

BARBER

Ali *Barber*

Taken from, Ali Baba and the 40 Thieves, the Arabian Nights.

Ali Baba (علي بابا ʿAlī Bābā), is a character from the folk tale Ali Baba and the Forty Thieves (علي بابا والأربعون لصا).

It is one of the most familiar "Arabian Nights" tales, although the most violent aspects of the story are usually suppressed, particularly when performed or broadcast for children.

BARKER

Ronnie *Barker*

Comedy again... no surprise.

Used as a nickname associated with the comedian, Ronald William George Barker, OBE.

Ronnie was known for his roles in comedy television series such as Porridge, The Two Ronnie's and Open All Hours.

He began acting in repertory theatre and discovered he was best suited to comic roles. His first success was at the Oxford Playhouse in Tom Stoppard's 'The Real Inspector Hound'.

His television break came in the satirical series, 'The Frost Report', where he met Ronnie Corbett. The pair found fame with 'The two Ronnie's' show.

He mostly wrote comedy under his own name, although he adopted pseudonyms his written work after 1968, *including "Gerald Wiley"*, to avoid pre-judgments of his writing talent.

He won four BAFTA's for best light entertainment performance and received an OBE in 1978.

He died of heart failure on 3 October 2005, aged 76.

BATES

1, Basher *Bates*

Notoriety is probably why this name became popular with Matelots. In a way, the revulsion of this man's act was a prime reason for bestowing it on a fellow seaman.

Bates was a Protestant in Shankill Road, Belfast, from where he became a member of the Ulster Volunteer Force (UVF).

Bates was recruited into the Shankill Butchers gang in 1975 by its notorious ringleader, Lenny Murphy.

He became a 'sergeant' in the gang. It is reported Bates was a participant in killing Catholics when they were abducted by fellow Shankill Butcher, William Moore in his Black Taxi cab.

2, Master (masta) *Bates*

Play on words, one which leaves little to the imagination.

BELL

1, Daisy *Bell.*

Taken from the song (written in 1892) by Harry Dacre, called 'Daisy Bell', but often referred to as 'A Bicycle Built for Two'.

Daisy, Daisy, give me your answer do
I'm half-crazy all for the love of you
It won't be a stylish marriage
I can't afford a carriage
But you'll look sweet upon the seat
Of a bicycle built for two

There is a flower within my heart
Daisy, Daisy
Planted one day by a glancing dart
Planted by Daisy Bell

Whether she loves me or loves me not
Sometimes it's hard to tell
Yet I am longing to share the lot
Of beautiful Daisy Bell
Daisy, Daisy, give me your answer do

I'm half-crazy all for the love of you

It won't be a stylish marriage

I can't afford a carriage

But you'll look sweet upon the seat

Of a bicycle built for two

When the road's dark, we can both despise

Policemen and lamps as well

There are bright lights in the dazzling eyes

Of beautiful Daisy Bell

Daisy, Daisy, give me your answer do

I'm half-crazy all for the love of you

It won't be a stylish marriage

I can't afford a carriage

But you'll look sweet upon the seat

Of a bicycle built for two

The song was inspired by *Daisy Greville, the Countess of Warwick*, who was one of the many mistresses of King Edward VII.

As an added note, it is the earliest song sung using computer speech synthesis, later referenced in the film 2001: A Space Odyssey.

2, Dinger *Bell.*

3, Jingles *Bell*

Both self-evident.

BENNET

Wiggy *Bennet*

There are three possibilities here,

1, An early 20th-century playboy with links to journalism called Gordon 'Wiggy' Bennet,

'Wiggy' effectively founded international motor racing through his sponsorship of the Bennett Trophy races which ran from 1900 to 1905.

(That is years, not Jacks 24hr clock or it would have been a very short competition).

Bennet sponsored trophies for powered air racing and long-distance hot-air ballooning. The international Gordon Bennett balloon race continues to this day.

The phrase "*Gordon Bennett*" often used as a mild expletive.

2, 'Wiggy' is also a corruption of 'Burnett', naval slang for hair during the late 1940s to mid-1950s.

Possibly a misinterpretation of the Cockney rhyming slang 'Barnett' (*Barnett Fair*) = hair.

Barnet Fair is an annual horse fair held near Mays Lane, Barnet, England, on the first Monday in September. (*Barnet Fair and market were granted a charter by Queen Elizabeth I in 1588.*)

The band Steely Span recorded a song called Barnet Fair in 1980:

Once a year when the winter's calling
Birds fly south and the leaves are falling down
Just beyond the town, the meadow where a campfire's burning
Wakes in the morning to the music of the big fairground

Coming from the east, coming from the west, all the gypsies are gathering

Just another town on the road for the travelling man

Follow me, boys, won't you follow me to Barnet Fair?

Follow on children won't you follow me to Barnet Fair?

If I show you the way won't you come along today?

Everyone you know will be there

Follow me, boys, won't you follow me to Barnet Fair

Leave the factory, leave the field

Word is abroad that the fair arrives today

Come on from the dusty loom and the rusty plough

Join the procession, I can hear it come this way

Come and see the juggler, come and see the fiddler

See the horses and the dancing bear

Come and see the pretty lasses with the coloured ribbons in their hair

Follow me, boys, won't you follow me to Barnet Fair?

Follow on children won't you follow me to Barnet Fair?

If I show you the way won't you come along today?

Everyone you know will be there

Follow me, boys, won't you follow me to Barnet Fair

3, The third possibility is 'Wiggy' Bennet became an affectionate name for a wig maker who supplied the Admiralty.

As popular and widespread as this version may be, it has no proven historical record associating it directly with the RN.

BERESFORD

Charlie *Beresford*

This one has some interesting facts and is directly connected with the Royal Navy.

Admiral Lord Charlie Beresford was the arch-rival of Admiral Jackie Fisher, during the early twentieth century.

To use his full name, Charles William de la Poer Beresford, 1st Baron Beresford, GCB, GCVO, Admiral and Member of Parliament, was the second son of John Beresford, the fourth Marquess of Waterford.

Beresford combined two careers, the Navy and serving as a member of parliament, giving him a reputation of hero in battle and as the champion of the navy in the House of Commons.

His later career encompassed an ongoing dispute with Admiral of the Fleet, Sir John Fisher regarding the reforms championed by Fisher, which included sweeping away many traditions and introducing new technologies.

(*Sounds somewhat familiar.*)

Fisher, who was slightly senior to Beresford and more successful, stopped Beresford's rise to the highest office in the navy of becoming the First Sea Lord.

It is quite obvious Jack should grasp the opportunity to link the name Charlie/Charly with anyone called Beresford from this time onwards.

BIRD

1, Dicky *Bird.*

Harold Dennis "Dickie" Bird, OBE, hails from Staincross in the West Riding of Yorkshire.

He is a well-known, respected and loved cricket commentator.

In 2014, Yorkshire Cricket Club voted Dickie Bird to be the club's president.

On his appointment Bird stated,

"Never in my wildest dreams did I think I would become the president of the greatest cricket club in the world".

2, Tweety (tweets) *Bird.*

Often a child's *(read Matelots!)* name for a bird.

BLAKE/ BLAKEMAN

Snaky *Blake*

From the Cruiser of the same name.

HMS Blake, (C99), was known as the Snaky Blake because of the strange corkscrew movement it made when sailing. This was due to the length of the ship (600ft) combined with its width of 60ft, which made Blake's wake 'snake'.

HMS Blake, a light cruiser of the Tiger class, was the last traditional Royal Navy gun armed cruisers. She was named after Robert Blake, a 17th-century admiral, known as the "*Father of the Royal Navy*".

Blake was withdrawn from service in 1979, she was the last ship in the Royal Navy to fire a six-inch gun.

BODY (BODDY)

Dogs *Body. (dog/doggy)*

Deffo Pusser by origin

1, Dogs *Body.*

There is a dish made from dried peas and eggs which is boiled in a bag. The resulting concoction is known as '*Pease pudding'* and it became a staple food of the Royal Navy during the 19th century.

Sailors nicknamed this item 'dog's body.'

2, Dogs *Body.*

(*Not totally unconnected to the above.*)

In the early part of the 20th century, junior officers and midshipmen who performed jobs the senior officers did not want to do became known as 'dogsbodies'.

The term became more common in non-naval usage during the 1930's when it was applied to general labourers and menial workers.

> *The term 'dogsbody' is not always derogatory. History records several people choosing the name as their callsign.*
>
> *The most famous of these is probably Douglas Bader, an RAF fighter pilot during the Second World War.*

BOLT

1, Bernie *Bolt*

Jack loved his television shows.

From the catchphrase, 'Bernie the Bolt'.

'Bernie', a Birmingham man who gained fame on the TV game show 'The Golden Shot', which was presented by Bob Monkhouse.

Bernie was a *'behind-the-scenes worker'*, whose name was John Baker. He fell into the role of loading a crossbow for contestants to aim and gained the nom de plume of 'Bernie'.

It brought him unexpected celebrity status and sackfuls of fan mail.

2, Usain *Bolt* (Modern)

I must admit am pre-empting this one as I have not heard anyone endowed with this nickname at the time of writing, but I honestly believe by the time this book is published there shall be at least one matelot who will bear this moniker.

Usain St Leo Bolt OJ CD is a retired Jamaican sprinter and the world record holder in the 100 metres, 200 metres and 4 × 100 metres relay. *(At the time of writing.)*

His reign as Olympic Games champion in these events spans three Olympics.

Due to his achievements and dominance in sprint competition, he is widely considered to be the greatest sprinter of all time.

BOND

There are two choices for this one. I think both are correct as origins, as each is 'of its time'.

1, Brook *Bond.*

Brooke Bond & Company was founded, by a Lancastrian chap named Arthur Brooke, in 1845.

Arthur opened his first tea shop in 1869, on Market Street, in Manchester.

He decided on the name to convey his 'bond' to provide quality tea, hence 'Brooke Bond'. The firm expanded into wholesale tea sales in the 1870s.

Brooke Bond's most famous brand, PG Tips, was launched in 1930.

By 1957, Brooke Bond was the largest tea company in the world, with a one-third share of both the British and Indian tea markets.

2, James (Jimmy) *Bond*

&

3, Double Ooh *Bond*

The options are formed from the James Bond films off fictional British Secret Service agent, James Bond, whose character was created in 1953 by Ian Fleming.

Since Fleming's death in 1964, eight other authors have written authorised Bond novels or novelisations.

Bond is known by his code number, 007, (*hence the Double Ooh above*) and was supposedly a Royal Naval Reserve Commander.

Did you know?

Fleming based his creation by amalgamating the characteristics of several individuals he met during his service in the Naval Intelligence Division during the Second World War

Fleming admitting Bond

"James is a compound of all the secret agents and commando types I met during the war."

4, Pusser *Bond*

No authentic information, but possibly just Jack taking the p*ss mickey out of either of the above Bonds?

BONE

Johnny *Bone*

This one is well documented in Royal Naval archive recordings.

Tradition has it 'Johnny Bone' was an eminent Scrounger or Rabbitter.

(*Originally "rabbits" were things smuggled ashore. The name came from sailors who would take such illicit items as Rum or Tobacco ashore concealed inside a dead rabbit, hence the phrase "***Tuck its ears in***", when a Matelot is seen taking a package ashore.*)

The name comes from the Boatswain on Admiral Cornwallis's Flag Ship, HMS Neptune, who was notorious for making good deficiencies in his stores by stealing from other ships.

The Admiral is reported to have said to the Boatswain on one occasion:

"I trust, Mr. Bone, you will leave me with my anchors?"

BOOTH

Billy *Booth*

After William Booth, an English Methodist preacher and founder of The Salvation Army.

Founded in 1865 The 'Sally Army' spread from London to many parts of the world. It is one of the largest distributors of humanitarian aid.

In 2002, Booth was named among the 100 Greatest Britons in a BBC poll.

William Booth was the second son of five children born to Samuel Booth and his second wife, Mary Moss.

Booth's father was wealthy but, during William's childhood, the family descended into poverty.

In 1842, Samuel Booth, who could no longer afford his son's school fees, apprenticed the 13-year-old William Booth to a pawnbroker.

BRAY

1, Donkey *Bray.*

2, E-haw *Bray.*

Do you need this explaining?

BRITTON

Battler *Britton*

(*A contraction of 'Battle of Britain'*)

Reference to the Battle of Britain during WWII, between the RAF and the Luftwaffe.

It was the first major military campaign fought entirely by air forces.

The British officially recognise the battle's duration as being from 10 July until 31 October 1940, which overlaps the period of large-scale night attacks known as the Blitz, which lasted from 7 September 1940 to 11 May 1941.

German historians do not accept this subdivision and regard the battle as a single campaign, lasting from July 1940 to June 1941, inclusive of the Blitz.

On 1 August, the Luftwaffe was directed by the German High Command to achieve air superiority over the RAF.

12 days later, it shifted attacks to RAF airfields and infrastructure.

As the battle progressed, the Luftwaffe targeted factories involved in aircraft production and strategic infrastructure.

Eventually, it resorted to carpet bombing on areas of political significance and civilian homes.

BROOKE (Brook)

Rajah *Brookes.*

This is a true 'did you know' revelation.

In the mid-19th century, until the Japanese occupation of Sarawak during WW2, the Brooke family controlled the territory of Sarawak in the East Indies.

They were colloquially known as the 'White Rajahs'

It was a dynastic monarchy of the Brooke family who founded and ruled the Kingdom of Sarawak, located on the island of Borneo, from 1841 to 1946.

The first ruler was Mr. James Brooke. He was given the territory, as an independent kingdom in 1841, as a reward for assisting the Sultan of Brunei fight piracy and insurgents.

Through male lineage, as dictated in the will of Sir James Brooke, the 'White Rajahs' continued until 1964 when the grandnephew of Sir James ceded all rights to the United Kingdom.

His nephew was the legal heir to the throne and objected to the cession, as did most of the Sarawak members of the Council Negri.

But to no avail.

BROWN/BROWNE

Grab a cuppa, there is a large assortment of characters here, any of which could be the origin, possibly several, for several various nominees.

Number 5 in this section is my own favourite contender.

1, Buster *Brown.*

As the mascot of the Brown Shoe Company in 1904, Buster Brown, (his sweetheart Mary Jane and his dog Tige, an American Pit Bull Terrier), were well-known in American by the early 20th century.

The comic strip began in the New York Herald in 1902.

When Outcault joined William Randolph Hearst's newspaper empire in 1906, a court battle ensued. Outcult continued his strip without a title name, while the Herald made their own version using other artists.

The latter lasted until 1911 or so, and Outcault's version until at least 1921.

2, Bomber *Brown*

Boxer, Joseph Louis Barrow, best known as Joe Louis was nicknamed "Brown Bomber".

Joe reigned as the world heavyweight champion from 1937 to 1949. He is considered one of the great heavyweights of all time.

Joes' championship reign lasted 140 consecutive months, during which he participated in 26 championship fights.

OR...

3, Because English sportsmen were popular, much as they are today...

George 'Bomber' Brown was an English professional footballer who played most of his career with Huddersfield Town.

A centre-forward, George became the highest ever goal-scorer for Huddersfield Town with 159 goals; 142 in the League in 213 appearances and 17 from 16 outings in the FA Cup.

George was signed directly from his amateur coal mining pit team in 1921, eventually being sold to Aston Villa in August 1929 for £5,000.

During his career, George scored 273 goals in 440 games, between 1921 and 1938.

He gained 9 England caps.

4, Charlie *Brown.*

Charlie Brown, the prime protagonist in the comic strip Peanuts, which is syndicated in daily and Sunday newspapers in numerous countries all over the world.

The character's creator, Charles M. Schulz, said of the character that,

"He must be the one who suffers because he is a caricature of the average person. Most of us are much more acquainted with losing than winning."

5, Billy *Brown.*

William Brown (*also known in Spanish as Guillermo Brown*) was an Irish-born Argentine admiral.

Brown's victories in the Independence War, the Cisplatine War and the Anglo-French blockade of the Río de la Plata earned the respect and appreciation of the Argentine people and he is still regarded as one of Argentina's national heroes.

Creator and first admiral of the country's maritime forces, he is commonly known as the "father of the Argentine Navy".

(*If he had not released Garibaldi, modern-day Italy would doubtfully exist.)*

5, Winkle *Brown.*

Captain Eric Melrose "Winkle" Brown, CBE, DSC, AFC, Hon FRAeS, RN was a British Royal Navy officer and test pilot who flew 487 types of aircraft, more than anyone else in history.

He was the most decorated pilot in the history of the Royal Navy.

Brown holds the world record for the most aircraft carrier deck take-offs and landings performed *(2,407 and 2,271 respectively)* and achieved several "firsts" in naval aviation, including the first landings on an aircraft carrier of a twin-engine aircraft, an aircraft with a tricycle undercarriage, a jet-propelled aircraft, and rotary-wing aircraft.

He also flew almost every category of Royal Navy and RAF aircraft: glider, fighter, bomber, airliner, amphibian, flying boat and helicopter. During World War II, he also flew many types of captured German, Italian, and Japanese aircraft, including new jets and rocket planes.

He remained a pioneer of jet technology into the post-war era.

BUNN

Sticky *Bunn.*

All cakes & sweet pastries are sticky buns to a matelot. See *'The Pussers Cook Book'* on Amazon.co.uk

BUTLER

1, Rab *Butler.*

(Rab is a Scottish enunciation of Rob/Robert)

Conservative Minister 1950s/60s. Became Chancellor of the Exchequer in 1951.

Richard Austen Butler, Baron Butler of Saffron Walden, KG, CH, PC, DL, known as R. A. Butler and familiarly known from his initials as RAB, was a prominent British Conservative politician.

The Times obituary called him

"*the creator of the modern educational system, the key figure in the revival of post-war Conservatism, arguably the most successful chancellor since the war and unquestionably a Home Secretary of reforming zeal."*

He was one of his party's leaders in promoting the Post-war consensus through which the major parties largely agreed on the main points of domestic policy until the 1970s, sometimes known as "Butskellism" from an elision of his name with that of his Labour counterpart Hugh Gaitskell.

2, Claude *Butler.*

Famous British bicycle manufacturer.

Claud Butler, the son of a worker in the silk industry who thought his son would follow him into the trade.

Instead, Claude developed an interest in cycles after delivering bottles of medicine for a doctor in south London on a bicycle.

He joined Balham cycling club and worked for Halford Cycle Company until February 1928, when he opened his own cycle shop in Clapham Junction where he began building his own bicycle frames.

The weekly magazine, The Bicycle, said:

"Ideas, practical innovations, use of the latest machinery brought "C.B." bicycles well to the fore in the lightweight industry. Claud Butler accomplished many fine technical achievements and pioneered many of the present-day developments."

Claude's innovations include the origination of the upright bicycle, the development of the short wheel-base tandem and the introduction of three speeds on tricycles.

The cycles were known for features such as bronze-weld construction and decorative lugs.

C

Charlie

CAIN (CANE/KAIN)

Cobber *Cane*.

Jack is never too worried about the correct spelling of a man's name if it sounds right when spoken.

Now, there was this chap named Edgar James 'Cobber' Kain, DFC, a New Zealand fighter ace in the Royal Air Force during the Second World War.

Kain was a piolet in the Advanced Air Striking Force (AASF), gaining his first victory in November 1939. A second followed days later. In March his fifth victory saw him become the first fighter ace (*a pilot credited with five or more enemy aircraft 'kills'*).

The Phoney War ended in May 1940 as the Battle of France and the Low Countries began. Within 17 days, Kain claimed a further 12 victories. His early success meant he quickly became a household name.

Said to be physically exhausted, Kain was ordered to return home on the 7th of June 1940.

He took off in a Hurricane and performed a series of low-level aerobatics, over Échemines airfield, as a goodbye gesture to his fellow pilots, unfortunately, he crashed and died instantly.

At that time Kain held the rank of flying officer and was credited with 17 aerial victories against the Luftwaffe. He was WW2's first recipient of the DFC.

CARPENTER

1, Chippy *Carpenter*

Often a carpenter is referred to as a 'chippy' because they make chips when they chop wood.

Out of interest...

Henry McNish, often referred to as Harry McNeish or by the nickname 'Chippy', was the carpenter on Sir Ernest Shackleton's Imperial Trans-Antarctic Expedition of 1914–1917.

Along for the ride was 'Mrs Chippy', the tabby cat who formed part of the ship's company when they set sail from the East India Docks in London on 1 August 1914.

Despite the name 'Mrs Chippy,' the cat was a tough tomcat from Glasgow. It is said he belonged to Henry the ship's master shipwright... hence the cat was nicknamed 'Mrs Chippy' regardless of the poor tom's gender.

2, Karen *Carpenter*

Karen Anne Carpenter, along with her brother Richard was the singing duo known simply as 'The Carpenters'.

Karen was critically acclaimed for her contralto vocals while her drumming was praised by contemporary musicians and peers.

She suffered from anorexia nervosa, which was never disclosed until later in her career.

Karen died, age 32, on February 4th, 1983 from heart failure related to her illness. Her death helped increased awareness of eating disorders.

Did you know?

While the Carpenters were on hiatus in the late 1970s, Karen recorded a solo album?

It was never released until after her death.

CARTER

Nick *Carter*

There are many Matelots who have fantasised about being a secret agent at some point in their career; for many, it has been Nick Carter who they would have loved to imitate.

Nick Carter is a fictional character who began as a pulp-fiction private detective in 1886 and has appeared in a variety of formats for more than a century.

Nick Carter - 'Killmaster', is a series of spy adventures published from 1964 until 1990.

At least 261 novels were published, ye no author is credited for any of the books. Among the authors who wrote, Nick Carter stories are Michael Avallone, Valerie Moolman, Manning Lee Stokes, Dennis Lynds, Gayle Lynds, Robert J. Randisi, David Hagberg, and Martin Cruz Smith.

The 'Nick Carter' is a house pseudonym of the character who serves as Agent N3 of AXE, a fictional US government agency.

One could say Nick Carter is not dissimilar to James Bond, but the stories tend not to use many gadgets, preferring high octane action sequences along with a liberal sprinkling of sexual encounters, many which are described in some detail.

Possibly one reason for Nick Carter's popularity?

2, Peanuts *Carter*

Itself a nickname for a former American president.

Born in 1924, James Earl Carter, Jr. grew up on a peanut farm, a crop which was to have a great impact on his life.

He served as the 39th President of the United States from 1977 to 1981.

Previously he was the 76th Governor of Georgia, after two terms in the Georgia State Senate.

CARTWRIGHT

Ben *Cartwright*

This was an 'unmissable' show in any mess.

Benjamin or "Ben" Cartwright is one of the main characters of the TV series Bonanza. Bonanza first aired in 1959 and is being repeated today.

Did you know?

The word 'Bonanza' derives from 19th century Spanish.

It translates as 'fair weather, prosperity', from the Latin word 'bonus' meaning good.

CASEY

Ginger *Casey*

Another peculiarly British name

Casey is a common variation of the Irish Gaelic Cathasaigh/Cathaiseach, meaning vigilant or watchful. Hence O'Cathasaigh or Mac Cathaiseach. 'O' meaning 'of' or descendant and 'Mac/Mc meaning 'son of'...

There are not many Casey's from Irish descent who do not sport a copper bonnet.

Therefore 'Ginger' or 'Ginge' is usually an appropriate and fitting name.

One (in)famous Casey, who could have given early Royal Naval Casey's their name, was John Keegan Casey who was known as the 'Poet of the Fenians'.

He was a Republican poet, novelist and orator.

He wrote the song **'The Rising of the Moon'** when he was 15 years of age.

The song Commemorates the 1798 Irish Rebellion.

THE ANDREW, JACK & JENNY

THE RISING OF THE MOON

And come tell me Sean O'Farrell, tell me why you hurry so
Hush a bhuachaill, hush and listen and his cheeks were all aglow
I bear orders from the captain, get you ready quick and soon
For the pikes must be together at the rising of the moon
At the rising of the moon, at the rising of the moon
For the pikes must be together at the rising of the moon
And come tell me Sean O'Farrell, where the gathering is to be
At the old spot by the river quite well known to you and me

One more word for signal token, whistle out the marching tune
With your pike upon your shoulder at the rising of the moon
At the rising of the moon, at the rising of the moon
With your pike upon your shoulder at the rising of the moon

Out from many a mud walled cabin eyes were watching through the night
Many a manly heart was beating for the blessed morning's light
Murmurs ran along the valley to the banshee's lonely croon
And a thousand pikes were flashing by the rising of the moon

By the rising of the moon, by the rising of the moon

And a thousand pikes were flashing by the rising of the moon

All along that singing river, that black mass of men was seen

High above their shining weapons flew their own beloved green

Death to every foe and traitor, whistle out the marching tune

And hoorah me boys for freedom 'tis the rising of the moon

'Tis the rising of the moon, 'tis the rising of the moon

And hoorah me boys for freedom 'tis the rising of the moon

CASSIDY

1, Hopalong *Cassidy*

A great name for anyone with a limp. Probably not 'PC' nowadays, but back in the 'good 'ole days' anyone's slight imperfection would be pounced on with much merriment and joy.

Hopalong Cassidy, or Hop-along Cassidy, is a fictional cowboy hero created in 1904 by the author Clarence E. Mulford, who wrote a series of popular short stories and novels based on the character.

Modern descendants of the author argue the stories and name are based on a real person who was a friend of the author.

In his early writings, Mulford portrayed the character as a rude, dangerous and rough-talking person with a wooden leg, which caused him to walk with a little 'hop', hence the nickname.

2, Butch *Cassidy*

How could any 'true blue' matelot not have an oppo called 'butch'?

Butch Cassidy, on the other hand, was a real person. His full name was Robert Leroy Parker.

In 1900 he partnered with Harry Longabaugh, (nicknamed as the "Sundance Kid"). They rob banks and trains, forming a group of outlaws they called the 'Wild Bunch'.

They eluded police by escaping to South America.

BUT...

In 1906, they returned to crime.

This is where it all gets a bit... um... hazy, as reports and records are patchy and often fake.

A: It has been said the pair were trapped and killed by police in Bolivia in 1908.

B: Some evidence suggests Cassidy faked his death, returning to the United States under the name of William T. Phillips and worked as a mechanist, before dying of cancer in Spokane, Washington in 1937.

Whatever the truth, Butch Cassidy's and Sundance are immortalized in the 1969 movie 'Butch Cassidy and the Sundance Kid', starring Paul Newman and Robert Redford.

CASTLE

1, Bouncy *Castle.*

Oh, come on... it's a children's party toy... that's it... nothing more.

2, If you have ginger hair, you may get Sandy... Sandy Castle, but it seems rare.

CHANDLER

Jeff *Chandler.*

Jeff Chandler, whose real name is Ira Grossel, is an actor, film producer and singer. He is best remembered for playing Cochise in Broken Arrow (1950).

CHAMBERLAIN

Nevil *Chamberlain.*

So-called, after Arthur Neville Chamberlain, of the Conservative Party.

He served as Prime Minister from May 1937 to May 1940.

Chamberlain is remembered for his foreign policy of seeking appeasement with the Nazi Party and for signing the Munich Agreement in 1938, conceding German-speaking Sudetenland, which was a region of Czechoslovakia to Germany.

However, when Adolf Hitler invaded Poland in 1939, Chamberlain led Britain through the first eight months of WW2.

Bowel cancer struck soon after his resignation, forcing him to leave Winston Churchill's coalition government. On his deathbed, he gathered the strength to whisper, "*approaching dissolution brings relief*".

CHAPMAN

Charlie *Chapman.*

Uncertainty abounds regarding this connotation. But one possibility is...

There was a fellow named Charles Thomas "Charlie" Chapman, he was an Australian rules footballer, with Fitzroy in the Victorian Football League (VFL).

Chapman, a ruckman and centre half-forward, appeared for Fitzroy in the 1924 finals. He played in two semi-finals and kicked two goals in each game, making him the first Fitzroy player to make his league debut in a final's series.

Charlie represented Victoria at interstate football on 10 occasions, including matches in the 1930 Adelaide Carnival.

NOTE:

Of course, this nickname could also be a result of Jack's ineptitude and was foisted on 'Chapman's' as a corruption of 'Chaplin' (silent films?)

CHASE

1, Charlee *Chase.*

I can't see Jack attesting to this one... then maybe I can... !

Charlee Chase, the stage name of an American pornographic actress.

She is credited with more than 400 films.

Charlee won an AVN Award and an XRCO Award and received nominations for the XBIZ Awards and Urban X Awards.

In September 2011, she was involved in a scandal with some Los Angeles City firemen. During a film scene, shot a couple of years earlier, Charlee can be seen next to a fire truck, exposing herself and inviting passers-by to fondle her.

(Nope, nothing to do with Jack... unless you were there?)

CLARK(E)

1, Nobby *Clark.*

This name has several urban folklores, each attesting to the origination of 'Nobby'. While there are some similarities, not one can be proven as the definitive answer.

A, because of the Industrial Revolution many commoners became wealthy and, to identify with their new-found wealth, some changed the spelling of their names. Smith became Smythe, Brown added an 'e' to gentrify the name as did many Clark's so it became Clarke. The relatives, who did not benefit from this 'new money', referred to their 'stuck-up' relations as the nobs or the Nobby Clarks.

B, *A similar version is...* No matter how poorly paid, Clarks were required to dress smartly like a 'nob' (*toff or well-to-do*), thus a Clark was often referred to as a 'Nobby Clark'.

C, *An alternative view...* With reference to the employment of a clerk. When clerks wrote with quill pens, they often did so for 10 hours a day, 6 days a week. Eventually, this caused callouses and arthritic knuckles. (*Fingers with knobs on*).

D, *the last option which deserves any attention is...*

So-called because, in olden times not so many people were educated to read and write, they employed the use of scribes to write on their behalf.

These scribes wore a type of apron with many small pockets for holding various bottles of inks and other writing paraphernalia, these items formed knobs in the scribes (clerks) aprons, giving rise to the nickname of Nobby/Knobby.

(*Humm... possibly... or not*).

2, Petula *Clark.*

There can be little argument over this one.

Petula Clark who, by the way, was born Sally Olwen Clark, was a singer, actress and composer.

Petula's career began on BBC Radio during World War II.

During the 1950s she started recording in French, gaining international success with the songs "The Little Shoemaker", "Baby Lover", "With All My Heart" and "Prends Mon Cœur".

During the 1960s she became known for her upbeat hits which include "Downtown", "This Is My Song" and "Don't Sleep in the Subway".

In America, Petula became "*the First Lady of the British Invasion*". To date, she has sold more than 68 million records worldwide.

COLE

1, Smokey *Cole.*

Play on words Cole - coal, smoke... oh, come on.

2, Nat *Cole.*

Of course, this is after the American singer, Nat King Cole, who was an American jazz pianist and vocalist.

Nat recorded over one hundred hit songs and his trio became the model for many jazz ensembles.

He also acted in several films, on television and performed on Broadway.

He was the first black man on American TV to host his own series.

COLLINS

This name was fascinating to research.

1, Jumper *Collins.*

The origin of name 'jumper', when associated with the surname Collins, has been lost, but a little... well, quite a lot of research enlightened me to what is most probably the connective origin, although no official academic has yet acknowledged its accuracy.

Think jumper... cardigan... sweater... seaman's jersey... and you are heading in the right direction.

By all accounts, the original Royal Navy's seaman's issue jumper was based on the traditional Irish fisherman's 'Coileán' knitting pattern.

Collins is a modern derivation of from the Gaelic 'Coileán'. It is Anglicized form of Gaelic Ó Coileáin and Mac Coileáin. a Patronymic from the Middle English personal name Col(l)in, a pet form of Coll, itself a short form of Nicholas.

Slops, it is said, listed the item in its usual way...

Example...

Boots - Marching - Black

Regarding seaman's jumpers...

Jumper - Collins – Blue

2, John *Collins.*

I may have tried a few, for research purposes only... of course.

A John Collins is a cocktail attested to in 1869, but its origin may be older if the information below is correct.

It is said the cocktail was created, named by and after, the headwaiter at Limmer's Old House in Conduit Street, Mayfair, a popular London hotel and coffee house in the late 1700's to the early 1800's.

The John Collins is a cocktail made from gin, lemon juice, sugar and carbonated water.

A recipe for a John Collins is featured in the Steward and Barkeeper's Manual of 1869:

A teaspoonful of powdered sugar

The juice of half a lemon

A wine glass of Old Tom Gin

A bottle of plain soda

Shake up or stir up with ice.

Add a slice of lemon peel to finish.

Drinks historian David Wondrich speculates the *'original recipe' (?)* was introduced to New York in the 1850s, saying it is like gin punches served at London clubs like the Garrick, during the first half of the 19th century.

He suggests these drinks would have "*gin, lemon juice, chilled soda water, and maraschino liqueur,*" in their make-up.

The specific call for 'Old Tom gin' in the 1869 recipe is the possibility for the cocktails name change to "Tom Collins". (Jerry

Thomas's 1876 recipe). The "John Collins" refers to a "Tom Collins" made with whiskey instead of gin.

(Earlier versions probably used Hollands Gin).

There are few, if any sailors of the Royal Navy, who have not indulged in at least one Tom/John Collins's somewhere in the world.

FACT:

The finest John Collins ever served anywhere on this planet was in the Fleet Club, Grand Harbour, Malta, in the mid-1970's.

COOPER

1, Mini *Cooper.*

The Mini is a production car introduced during the 1960's.

John Cooper, the owner of the Cooper Car Company and designer and builder of Formula One and rally cars, saw the potentiall of the original Mini for competition and worked with Issigonis, the designer of the original Mini to create the Mini Cooper.

2, Duff *Cooper.*

Even politics did not dissuade Jack from adopting names.

The first Viscount Norwich, known as Duff Cooper, was a British Conservative Party politician, diplomat and author whose full name was Alfred Duff Cooper.

Cooper put his trust in the League of Nations realising war with Germany was inevitable. He denounced the Munich agreement as meaningless, cowardly and unworkable and, in protest, resigned from cabinet.

When (*Winston*) Churchill became prime minister in May 1940, reinstated Cooper as Minister of Information.

From 1941, Cooper served in numerous diplomatic roles. Most importantly as British representative to de Gaulle's Free France (1943–44) and ambassador to France from 1944–48.

CORNISH

This one is close to many sailors' hearts.

Pasty/Oggie *Cornish.*

Documented as an integral part of the British diet since the 13th Century; at which time it was being devoured by the upper class and royalty, with fillings of stewed venison, beef, lamb and seafood, (like eels).

There is no record of the pasty being eaten by miners or farm workers before the 17th century.

Legend has it, wives of Cornish tin miners enclosed an 'all-in-one meal' in thick pastry, crimped along one edge, to provide sustenance for workers at depths where it was not possible to reach the surface to eat a meal.

It has been said a good pasty could survive being dropped down a mine shaft. (*I wonder?*)

One school of thought is, the thick twisted crust served as a means of holding the pasty with dirty hands without contaminating the meal, especially when in contact with arsenic, which is commonly found in/with tin.

However, this is disputed, for what hungry minor would waste (*almost*) perfectly edible food. They breathed in the Arsenic laden air all day and lived with it on their clothing, so a little ingested on a piece of pastry was of no concern.

CRABB

Proper Pusser this one...

Buster *Crabb*.

Lionel Kenneth Phillip Crabb, or 'Buster' Crabb, was a Royal Navy frogman and MI6 diver. He vanished during a reconnaissance mission of the Soviet cruiser Ordzhonikidze, when berthed at Portsmouth Dockyard in 1956.

Peter Wright, in his book 'Spycatcher', suggests Crabb was sent to investigate Ordzhonikidze's propeller, which was suspected to be of a new design, one Naval Intelligence wished to examine.

On 19 April 1956, Crabb dived into Portsmouth Harbour. It was the last time anyone saw him.

Crabb's belongings and the page of the hotel register, on which Crabb had written his name, disappeared from the Sally Port Hotels guest register.

On 29 April, Rear Admiral John Inglis, the Director of Naval Intelligence at the Admiralty announced Crabb's disappearance. He reported Crabb went missing during trials of secret underwater apparatus in Stokes Bay on the Solent.

The Soviets released a statement saying the crew *(of the Ordzhonikidze),* saw a frogman on 19 April.

Some newspapers speculated the Soviets captured Crabb and took him to the Soviet Union.

Prime Minister, Anthony Eden, told parliament it was not in the public interest to disclose the circumstances in which the frogman met his (*supposed*) end.

CROSS

Jumper *Cross.*

Try saying it quickly.

Oh, yer... I geddit now.

CROWN/CROWNE

1, Arfer *Crown.*

The half-crown was a denomination money, equivalent to two shillings and sixpence, or one-eighth of a pound.

The first half-crown was issued in 1549, during the reign of Edward VI and demonetised in January 1970, a year before we adopted decimal currency.

Did you know...

During the English Interregnum (1649–1660), a Republican half-crown was issued, bearing the arms of the Commonwealth of England.

When Oliver Cromwell became Lord Protector, half-crowns were struck with his image.

The half-crown coin did not display its value on the reverse until 1893.

2, Topper *Crown.*

A nickname itself for a wig and latter a trade name for a toupee.

D

Delta

DAVEY

Jack *Davey*

Probably...

Jack was a left-handed batsman who bowled left-arm fast-medium.

Davey had a successful career with Gloucestershire County Cricket Club from 1966 to 1978.

His name sometimes appeared in reports and on scorecards as J.J. Davey. The second 'J' was a creation by Alan Gibson whose campaign to exaggerate Davey's name to produce a commemorative tie, in Davey's testimonial season, with the initials JJ on it.

(Perhaps Alan Gibson already held a stock of ties with the letters 'JJ' printed on them in a 'lock-up garage' and was looking to offload them for a quick profit? Think 'Dell boy')

DAVIES

Dicky *Davies*.

This name was given after Richard "Dickie" Davies, who is best known for presenting World of Sport from 1968 until 1985.

Dickie's first job was as an announcer for Southern Television.

Davies worked on World of Sport (*initially called Wide World of Sports*) from 1965, as understudy to Eamonn Andrews, taking over as presenter in 1968 when Andrews left.

DAY

1, Happy *Day*

'Oh, Happy Day' is a 1967 gospel music arrangement of an 18th-century hymn which became an international hit after it was recorded by the Edwin Hawkins Singers,

"O Happy Day, That Fixed My Choice" by Philip Doddridge; The United Methodist Hymnal, No. 391

O happy day, that fixed my choice

On thee, my Saviour and my God!

Well may this glowing heart rejoice,

And tell its raptures all abroad.

Happy day, happy day,

When Jesus washed my sins away!

He taught me how to watch and pray,

And live rejoicing every day.

Happy day, happy day,

When Jesus washed my sins away.

2, Doris *Day*

Doris Day (Doris Mary Ann Kappelhoff), began her career as a big band singer recording her first hit "Sentimental Journey" in 1945.

Doris recorded over 650 songs from 1947 to 1967. Her film career began with 'Romance on the High Seas'. Her most successful films were bedroom comedies 'Pillow Talk' and 'Move Over, Darling'.

in 1968, she presented her TV series, The Doris Day Show, until 1973.

DEAN

Dixie/Dixy *Dean*.

(*William Ralph*) "Dixie" Dean was a top scoring Everton centre-forward.

Dean was from Birkenhead and started his career at Tranmere Rovers before moving to Everton.

His best season was 1927–28 when he scored a record 60 league goals.

A statue of Dean was unveiled outside Goodison Park in May 2001. Dean was the first Everton player to wear the number 9 shirt, which in later years would become iconic at the club.

DEMPSEY

Jack *Dempsey*

Boxers names have always been a favourite with sailors.

William Harrison "Jack" Dempsey, also known as "Kid Blackie" or the "The Manassa Mauler", was an American boxer from 1914 to 1927.

Dempsey was the world heavyweight champion from 1919 to 1926. His aggressive fighting style and exceptional punching power made Jack one of the most popular boxers in history.

Dempsey is ranked as tenth on The Ring magazine's list of all-time heavyweights and seventh in the Top 100 Greatest Punchers.

He was voted the as the greatest fighter of the past 50 years by the Associated Press in 1950.

DIAMOND

Legs *Diamond.*

Another must for Jack... a gangster of legend.

A 1920s/30s Notorious New gangster who became the subject of the film "The Rise and Fall of Legs Diamond".

He was an Irish American gangster operating in Philadelphia and New York City during Prohibition.

He was a bootlegger and associate of gambler Arnold Rothstein.

Diamond survived several attempts on his life between 1916 and 1931.

Dutch Schultz is said to have remarked to his own gang,

"Ain't there nobody that can shoot this guy so he don't bounce back?"

DITE

Arrol *Dite*.

I love this one.

The first production of epoxy resins was from De Trey Frères SA of Switzerland. The company licensed the process to Ciba AG in the 1940s.

Ciba launched the product 'Araldite' at the Swiss Industries Fair in 1945.

Ciba's epoxy business was sold in the late 1990s

It now belongs to UK Aero Research Limited. (ARL) - hence the name, ARaLdite.

E

Echo

EDWARDS

1, Bungy *Edwards*

There is no definitive for this nickname, although many suggestions have been put forward including the word 'Bungy' may be the name of a bung manufacturing company supplying the RN.

2, Another is 'Bungy' was an early schoolboy slang for a Rubber eraser. I guess we shall never know?

3, This is the most intriguing of all; even so, it could just be a shaggy dog told by sea daddies?

The dit follows these lines...

Two seamen chippies, Williams and Edwards were given the detail to construct the cask to house Nelson's body until it could be transported back home.

They dutifully did as they were ordered, but on learning the cask was to be filled with brandy, they added a device for extracting the spirit via the bung.

When the cask eventually arrived in England and was opened to extract Nelson's body, it was found his head was not covered and therefore not pickled, as was the rest of his body.

Some say it was evaporation, others that Edwards and Williams received a severe flogging.

Hence their names shall always be associated with Bungy.

(*Also see Williams*)

4, Daisy *Edwards.*

Unknown. I have not been able to find any recorded facts regarding this name paring.

If you have recorded facts, please let me know.

5, Eddie *Edwards.*

Simply name shortening (*a contraction*) or it could be... *(modern version).*

After Michael Edwards, known as "Eddie the Eagle " the skier who, in 1988, became the first competitor since 1928 to represent Great Britain in Olympic ski jumping, finishing last in both events.

He did, however, become the British ski jumping record holder!

In 2016, Eddie was played by Taron Egerton in the biographical film 'Eddie the Eagle'.

6, Spud *Edwards.*

Named after King Edward potatoes.

King Edward's have been cultivated in the UK since 1902, making it one of the oldest varieties still grown commercially.

ELLINGTON

Duke *Ellington.*

The jazz musician, Edward Kennedy "Duke" Ellington was based in New York City who rose to fame playing with his orchestra at the Cotton Club from in the 1920's

EVANS

1, Bandy Evans.

Unknown.

(*Vaguely possible it was used after an obscure cowboy character from a 1950's film. We all know a 'true blue western' was always an appreciated form of entertainment onboard*).

2, Crash *Evans.*

This name most likely became a popular nickname after the USS Frank E. Evans, DD-754, (*an Allen M. Sumner-class destroyer, named after Brigadier General Frank Evans, USMC, a leader of the American Expeditionary Force in France during World War I*), was sunk in a collision, 'CRASH', with the Australian aircraft carrier HMAS Melbourne in 1969.

3, Dorrie Evans.

After a prime character of the 1970's TV show 'Number 96', an Australian television soap opera.

'Number 96' spawned a feature film adaptation which became one of the most profitable Australian movies ever made.

This series was notable for sex scenes and nudity. It was the first soap opera in the world featuring a gay character.

4, Taff Evans.

But only if you are Welsh.

EWART

Nobby/Knobby *Ewart.*

A name with an amusing Pussers tale attached.

Admiral Charles Ewart, known as "Nobby" Ewart was the captain of H M S Melpomene from 1859 until 1862.

He was known for his personal neatness and his insistence regarding the appearance of everything on his ship.

One story is... objecting to the appearance of a goose, Admiral Nobby Ewart ordered the goose's bill and feet be blackened and its body whitewashed, in keeping with Navy regulations as to the birds colouring.

It was not long before this story circulated around the entire fleet.

When attending an opera in Malta, the story continues, as Nobby took his seat, a crowd of sailors in the gallery began calling "Who whitewashed the goose?"

In reply, the sailors on the opposite side of the theatre responded with, "Why, it was our Nobby Ewart."

The calling continued until the harassed Admiral walked out of the theatre.

While my research uncovered this most amusing story, you may notice it does not explain why the name 'Nobby' is linked to the name Ewart.

I thought I would share it with you anyway.

F

Foxtrot

FAILS

Aziz *Fails*

Originates from electrical 'fail-safe' switchgear often found in boats (*submarines*).

The switches are designed to fail in safe mode. The switch fails to an open or shut position, or as it is... as is... Aziz... geddit... oh never mind.

FAGIN

Patsy *Fagin*

Simply taken from the Irish folk song "Hello Patsy Fagin...

"Hello Patsy Fagan" you can hear the girls all cry

"Hello Patsy Fagan, you're the apple of me eye

You're a decent boy from Ireland, there's no one can deny

You're a rare'm tare'm devil may care,m decent Irish boy"

I'm working here in Glasgow, I've got a decent job

I'm carrying bricks and mortar and the pay is fifteen bob

I rise in the mornin', I get up with the lark

And when I'm walking' down the street, you can hear the girls remark

"Hello Patsy Fagan" you can hear the girls all cry

"Hello Patsy Fagan, you're the apple of me eye

You're a decent boy from Ireland, there's no one can deny

You're a rare'm tare'm devil may care,m decent Irish boy"

Well the day that I left Ireland, 'twas many months ago

I left my home in Ulster where the pigs and praties grow

But since I left old Ireland, it's always been my plan

To let you people, see that I'm a decent Irishman

"Hello Patsy Fagan" you can hear the girls all cry

"Hello Patsy Fagan, you're the apple of me eye

You're a decent boy from Ireland, there's no one can deny

You're a rare'm tare'm devil may care,m decent Irish boy"

Now if there's one among you would like to marry me

I'll take you to my little home across the Irish sea

I'll dress you up in satin and do I'll the best I can

And let the people see that I'm a decent Irishman.

FELL

Trip *Fell*

Surely this needs no explanation.

FIELDS

Gracie *Fields*

After the Actress who sang about an Aspidistra.

Dame Gracie Fields, (who was born Grace Stansfield), was made a Commander of the Order of the British Empire (CBE) for "services to entertainment" in 1938.

In 1979, seven months before her death on the Isle of Capri, she was invested a Dame by Queen Elizabeth II.

For years we had an aspidistra in a flower pot
On the whatnot, near the 'atstand in the 'all
It didn't seem to grow 'til one day our brother Joe
Had a notion that he'd make it strong and tall
So, he's crossed it with an acorn from an oak tree
And he's planted it against the garden wall
It shot up like a rocket, 'til it's nearly reached the sky
It's the biggest aspidistra in the world
We couldn't see the top of it, it got so bloomin' high
It's the biggest aspidistra in the world
When fathers had a snoot full at his pub, 'The Bunch of Grapes'
He doesn't go all fighting mad and getting into scrapes

No, you'll find him in his bear-skin playing Tarzan of the apes

Off the biggest aspidistra in the world

We have to get it watered by the local fire brigade

So, they put the water rates up half a crown

The roots stuff up the drains, grow along the country lanes

And they came up half a mile outside the town

Once we hired an auditorium for a hothouse

But a jealous rival went and burnt it down

The tomcats and their sweethearts love to spend their evenings out

Up the biggest aspidistra in the world

They all begin meowing when the buds begin to sprout

From the biggest aspidistra in the world

The dogs all come around for miles, a lovely sight to see

They sniff around for hours and hours and wag their tails with glee

So, I've had to put a notice up to say it's not a tree

It's the biggest aspidistra in the world.

FINCH

Robin *Finch.*

For absolutely no other reason that it is another birds name.

FISHER

Jackie/Jacky *Fisher*

Another great combination with true Pussers origin.

John Arbuthnot Fisher, the 1st Baron Fisher, commonly known as Jacky or Jackie Fisher was a British Admiral known for his efforts at naval reform.

His influence on the Royal Navy spanned over 60 years, starting in a navy of wooden sailing ships armed with muzzle-loading cannon and ending with one of steel-hulled battlecruisers, submarines and the first aircraft carriers.

The argumentative, energetic, reform-minded Fisher is considered the second most important figure in British naval history after Lord Nelson.

Fisher is celebrated as an innovator, strategist and developer of the navy, rather than a seagoing admiral involved in major battles, although he experienced all these things.

When appointed First Sea Lord in 1904, he removed 150 ships which were no longer useful and set about constructing modern replacements. He created the fleet which defended England against Germany during World War I.

FLOWER(S)

Flossie *Flower*

Most probably a term picked up by sailors on a run ashore, possibly in South Africa where the term 'Flossie' was used colloquially for a prostitute, or an *'overdressed eager woman'* (*circa 1910. Leechman. The tail of 98*)

Probable corruption of the word Floosie.

FUNNEL

Smokey *funnel.*

Self-explanatory.

FORD

1, Florrie *Ford.*

Born Flora May Augusta Flannagan she was an Australian vaudevillian entertainer.

From 1897 she lived and worked in the United Kingdom. She was one of the most popular stars of the early 20th-century music halls.

In 1903 she sang "Down at the Old Bull and Bush", a Grade II listed public house near Hampstead Heath in London.

Talk about the shade of the sheltering palm
Praise the bamboo tree with its wide-spreading charm,
There's a little nook down near old Hampstead Town,
You know the place it has one great renown,
Often with my sweetheart on a bright Summers day,
To the little pub there my footsteps will stray,
If she hesitates when she looks at the sign,
Promptly I whisper, "Now do not decline."
Come, come, come and make eyes at me
down at the Old Bull and Bush,
Da, da, da, da, da,
Come, come, drink some port wine with me,

Down at the Old Bull and Bush,

Hear the little German Band,

Da, da, da, da, da,

Just let me hold your hand dear,

Do, do come and have a drink or two

down at the Old Bull and Bush.

Do, do, come and have a drink or two

down at the Old Bull and Bush,

Bush, Bush.

Until the introduction of the English smoking ban on July 1, 2007, The Bull and Bush was one of the few completely smoke-free pubs in London.

Did you know...

Until the introduction of the English smoking ban on July 1, 2007, The Bull and Bush was one of the few completely smoke-free pubs in London.

2, Henry *Ford.*

Henry Ford captain of industry and a business magnate, founder of the Ford Motor Company and the development of assembly-line mass production.

Ford did not invent the automobile or the assembly line, but he developed and manufactured the first automobile many middle-class Americans could afford by utilising and improving the techniques.

As the owner of the Ford Motor Company, he became one of the richest and best-known people in the world.

Ford left most of his vast wealth to the Ford Foundation and arranged for his family to control the company permanently.

FOUNTAIN

Sprinkle *Fountain.*

You work it out.

FRANCIS

Connie *Francis*.

1950s/60s female pop singer, Connie Francis is an American pop singer of the late 1950s and 1960s.

Her chart success waned in the second half of the 1960s, Francis remained a top concert draw. Despite several severe interruptions in her career, she is still active as a recording and performing artist at the time of writing this book.

FREEMAN

Harry *Freeman.*

Two options here, although I favour the first as the origin regarding its Royal Naval use.

1, Harry Freeman, an English music hall performer of the Victorian era. First King Rat of the showbusiness charity the Grand Order of Water Rats.

Among his popular songs were 'Leicester Square' and 'The Giddy Little Girl said, "No!"'

His first appearance was in 1877 at a 'Free and Easy' held in the Imperial Theatre in Walsall. Harry made his London debut at 'Lusby's Music Hall' in 1881.

Harry Freeman died on 30 July 1922 following an abdominal operation at St Peter's Hospital in Covent Garden. He was buried in St Mary's Church, Handsworth in his native Birmingham.

2, Harry Septimus Freeman an Australian cricketer. He played four first-class cricket matches for Victoria between 1887 and 1889 and three for Queensland between 1893 and 1895.

G

GOLF

GALE/GAIL

Windy *Gale*

Play on words. Storm etc.

GARRET(T)

Pat *Garret*

Another western, always a favourite with Jack. This one has a legendary tale to boot.

Patrick Floyd Jarvis "Pat" Garrett an American Old (Wild) West lawman, bartender and customs agent who became renowned for killing Billy the Kid.

On December 15, 1880, Governor Wallace put a $500 reward on Billy's head. Pat Garrett then began his relentless pursuit.

On December 19, 1880, Garrett confronted Billy and his gang in Fort Sumner, New Mexico, killing Tom O'Folliard.

Billy and the rest of his gang escaped.

Garrett tracked the outlaws to Stinking Springs. After several days of siege, Garett's posse killed Charlie Bowdre, captured Billy the Kid, Dirty Dave Rudabaugh, Tom Pickett and Billy Wilson.

Billy the Kid was sentenced to hang in Lincoln, New Mexico on May 13, 1881. However, he escaped from jail killing two guards.

Garrett went after Billy once again.

He was at Peter Maxwell's ranch on July 14, 1881, questioning him about Billy's whereabouts.

Billy unexpectedly entered the room, not recognising Garrett in the dim indoors light asked "¿Quien es? ¿Quien es?" (*"Who is it? Who is it?)*

Garrett responded with two shots from his revolver, the first striking Billy's heart.

Billy the Kid was buried in a plot in-between his dead friends Tom O'Folliard and Charlie Bowdre the next day at Fort Sumner's cemetery.

GAY

1, Betsy *Gay*

Betsy Gay was in the 'Our Gang Comedies' beginning with 'Arbor Day' in 1935. The 'Our Gang Comedies' became known as 'Little Rascals' when the shows started running on TV.

Betsy lives in Bakersfield, California. Her husband Thomas Cashen ran Cashen Jewelers in Los Angeles on Olympic Boulevard.

He passed away in 2005.

2, Marvin *Gay.*

Marvin Gaye helped to shape the sound of Motown in the 1960s, His hits, including "Ain't That Peculiar", "How Sweet It Is (To Be Loved by You)" and "I Heard It Through the Grapevine".

During the 1970's Marvin recorded two concept albums, What's Going On and Let's Get It On.

He, along with Stevie Wonder, became the first artists in Motown to break away from a production company.

On April 1, 1984, Gaye's father, Marvin Gay Sr, shot and killed him.

3, Izzy *Gay*

Well, is he? (Izzy)... geddit?

GILBERT

Tosh *Gilbert*

I can find no association regarding the coupling of these names.

1, Tosh is often used as, "What a load of old tosh" meaning rubbish or untrue.

This is from records of the word 'Tosh' being used in Scotland during the 1770's to mean clean, trim.

From early 1800's London Slang references 'Tosh' to 'Valuables collected from drains'.

It is a possible evolution of these original meanings.

2, Alternatively, it is the Scottish reduced form of McIntosh, which is also established in northeastern Ulster.

3, An anglicised spelling of German 'Tosch' and the Slovenian 'Toš'. A derivative of the personal name Tomaž, as in Thomas.

GORDON

Flash *Gordon.*

Flash Gordon is the hero of a space adventure comic strip created by and originally drawn by Alex Raymond.

First published January 7, 1934, the strip was inspired by and created to compete with Buck Rogers.

GRANT

1, General *Grant.*

More western adventures.

General Ulysses S. Grant was the Commander-in-Chief of the Union forces during the American Civil War.

He was elected as the 18th President of the United States in 1868, serving from 1869 to 1877.

Commanding General, Grant, worked with President Abraham Lincoln to lead the Union Army to victory over the Confederacy.

Twice elected president, Grant led the Republicans in their effort to remove the vestiges of Confederate nationalism and slavery, protect African-American citizenship and civil rights, implement reconstruction and support economic prosperity.

2, Dolly *Grant.*

Yep... more cowboy stuff.

A character in the television series 'Rawhide'.

Dolly Grant was played by Brenda Scott and 'Rowdy Yates' by a relatively unknown actor called Clint Eastwood.

GRAVES

Digger *Graves.*

Oh, come on... this needs no explanation.

GRAY/GREY

Dolly *Grey.*

The name is taken from the song, "Goodbye Dolly Gray" written by William Cobb. It was a popular marching song during both the Boer War and the first world war, (WWI).

I have come to say goodbye, Dolly Gray,
It's no use to ask me why, Dolly Gray,
There's a murmur in the air, you can hear it everywhere,
it's the time to do and dare, Dolly Gray - so

Goodbye Dolly, I must leave you, though it breaks my heart to go,
Something tells me I am needed at the front to fight the foe,
See - the soldier boys are marching and I can no longer stay,
Hark - I hear the bugle calling, goodbye Dolly Gray.

Can't you hear the sound of feet, Dolly Gray,
Marching through the village street, Dolly Gray,
That's the tramp of soldiers' feet in their uniforms so neat,
So - goodbye until we meet, Dolly Gray. Goodbye Dolly Gray

Songs like Goodbye Dolly Gray demonstrate how music hall was used to gain patriotic support for the war. An early form of media propaganda.

Although this song originated during the American-Spanish War, it became a popular anthem in Music Halls during the Boer War.

The effectiveness of such controlled propaganda often referred to as a 'spin' nowadays, is shown in this songs re-emergence during World War 1.

GREEN

Jimmy *Green.*

1, Most probably taken from '*Jimmy Green and His Time Machine*', a children's TV series from 1968.

Jimmy Green travelled through time to various important historical events.

It was produced by Jess Yates. The puppets by Eric Bramall and Chris Somerville of the Harlequin Puppet Theatre in North Wales.

2, Sticky *Green*

Some sailors may know what these are if they ever visited certain drinking establishments.

A 'Sticky Green' is a non-alcoholic drink sailors are often coerced into buying 'bar girls' and charged extortionate prices.

Oh, it's also officers' slang for Crème de Menthe. Worlds apart, or maybe not?

GUNN

Ben *Gunn*

There is only one possible reason for this name... ooh arrgh, me hearties...

Ben Gunn is an ex-crewman of Captain Flint's, marooned for three years on *Treasure Island* by his crewmates, after his failure to find the treasure without the map.

During his time on the island, Ben develops a craving for cheese. Ben appears in the novel when met by Jim Hawkins.

Jim leaves Ben behind, escaping to Hispaniola on Ben's coracle.

Ben appears later in the book, he makes ghostly sounds delaying Long John Silver's men in their search for the hidden treasure.

They find where Flint's treasure was buried, but the treasure is gone.

Angered. the pirates attack Silver and Jim, but Ben Gunn and several others attack the pirates by surprise.

Silver surrenders to Dr. Livesey, promising to return to his "dooty".

They go to Ben Gunn's cave home, where the treasure is divided amongst Squire Trelawney and his loyal men, including Jim and Ben Gunn.

They then return to England, leaving pirates marooned on the island.

Being a 'proper' Jack, Gunn spends all his part of the treasure during a few days run ashore.

After which becomes a porter for the rest of his life.

And that crap is a best-selling book and film… what is this world coming too?

H

Hotel

HALL/HALLS

Nobby *Hall*

1, Some say this name is given for similar reasons as 'Nobby Clark'. (*See Nobby Clarke*)

BUT... my research shows a different and somewhat intriguing origin to this name and, knowing Jolly Jack Tar, I would bet my last Tot this is where the name Nobby (or Knobby) Hall came from.

The story goes like this...

Once upon a time... there was a young boy called Jack. He was sold by his parents, at the age of 7, for one guinea to a chimney sweep.

Later in life, Jack stole chimney pots and sold candles 'short of weight'... and got caught thieving.

In 1707 (*according to the Newgate calendar*), on his way up to the gallows on Holborn Hill, Jack was allowed to have a 'last tipple' at St. Giles public-house before being hanged at Tyburn.

Over a century later, Pitts printed a song called Jacks 'Last Goodbye' (*circa 1820*), which became a publicly popular street song. Later taken up by W.G. Ross, a well-known singer of the time, who sang it with great gusto at The Supper Rooms and The Cole Hole. (*At some unidentifiable point and for no apparent reason, the songs name was changed to Sam Hall and then to Nobby Hall*).

The songs Popularity lasted into the latter half of the nineteenth century which, it is suspected, is when the bawdy parody versions originated. These were mostly titled **'Nobby Hall'**.

It is not possible to give exact dates, as most bawdy songs had no written record until the middle of the 20th century.

The tune is that of the song Captain Kidd, who was hanged in 1701 and is related to that of Admiral Benbow, Ye Jacobites, Davy Lowton and many others.

As one would expect when evolving from a '*street*' song, via music halls and then to bawdy Ballards, 'Nobby Hall' has many versions, each claiming to be the original.

Here are three versions of 'Nobby Hall', followed by a more recent Bawdy one.

VERSION 1

His name was Nobby Hall, Nobby Hall, Nobby Hall
His name was Nobby Hall, Nobby Hall
His name was Nobby Hall and he only had one - arm
His name was Nobby Hall, Nobby Hall

They say he killed his wife, killed his wife, killed his wife
They say he killed his wife, killed his wife
They say he killed his wife, but it wasn't with a knife
They say he killed his wife, killed his wife

They sent him to the quad, to the quad, to the quad
They sent him to the quad, to the quad
They sent him to the quad 'cos he was a wicked - man
They sent him to the quad, to the quad

The judge's name was Hunt, name was Hunt, name was Hunt
The judge's name was Hunt, name was Hunt
The judge's name was Hunt and he was a silly - fool
The judge's name was Hunt, name was Hunt

The jailer's name was Jock, name was Jock, name was Jock

The jailer's name was Jock, name was Jock

The jailer's name was Jock and his keys hung from his - belt

The jailer's name was Jock, name was Jock

The parson came at last, came at last, came at last

The parson came at last, came at last

The parson came at last, with his prayer book up his - sleeve

The parson came at last, came at last,

So, they hung poor Nobby Hall, Nobby Hall, Nobby Hall

They hung poor Nobby Hall, Nobby Hall

They hung poor Nobby Hall, by his one remaining - arm

They hung poor Nobby Hall, Nobby Hall

VERSION 2:

His name was Nobby Hall, Nobby Hall,

His name was Nobby Hall, Nobby Hall,

His name was Nobby Hall and he only had one - - - finger,

His name was Nobby Hall, Nobby Hall.

He went to see his Granny, see his Granny,

He went to see his Granny, see his Granny,

He went to see his Granny, just to see her hairy - - - head,

He went to see his Granny, see his Granny.

He went to rob a bank, rob a bank,

He went to rob a bank, rob a bank,

He went to rob a bank, on the way he had a - - - sandwich,

He went to rob a bank, rob a bank.

The copper he came quick, he came quick,

The copper he came quick, he came quick,

The copper he came quick, he'd been playing with his - - - truncheon,

The copper he came quick, he came quick.

The Judge's name was Hunt, name was Hunt,

The Judge's name was Hunt, name was Hunt,

The Judge's name was Hunt, and he was a proper - - - qualified judge,

The Judge's name was Hunt, name was Hunt.

The Jury they were crackers, they were crackers,

The Jury they were crackers, they were crackers,

The Jury they were crackers, they were playing with their - - - pencils,

The Jury they were crackers, they were crackers.

So, they hung Nobby Hall, Nobby Hall,

So, they hung Nobby Hall, Nobby Hall,

So, they hung Nobby Hall, by his one and only - - - finger,

They hung Nobby Hall, Nobby Hall.

VERSION 3:

His name was Nobby Hall, Nobby Hall

His name was Nobby Hall, Nobby Hall

His name was Nobby Hall and he only had one ... finger

His name was Nobby Hall, Nobby Hall

He went to rob a bank, rob a bank

He went to rob a bank, rob a bank

He went to rob a bank rob a bank

He went to rob a bank

But he stopped to have a ..... sandwich

He went to rob a bank rob a bank

The policeman he came quick he came quick

The policeman he came quick he came quick

The policeman he came quick

and he hit him with his ..... truncheon

The policeman he came quick he came quick.

The judge's name was Enus it was Enus

The judge's name was Enus it was Enus

The judge's name was Enus

And he had a big white.....wig

The judge's name was Enus it was Enus.

They shoved him in the pit in the pit

They shoved him in the pit in the pit

They shoved him in the pit

And filled it up with... rose petals

They shoved him in the pit in the pit (in the pit)

This is one of the latest Bawdy Versions... the one you have been waiting for... and the one I am sure influenced Jack bestowing the name Nobby on anyone called Hall.

Oh, my name is knobby hall, knobby hall...
and I've only got one ball,
but tis better than none at all, fuck them all.

Oh, I've killed a man they said, so they said ...
crushed a gushed his bloody head
and I left him there for dead, fuck them all

Oh, they say that I must die, I must die...
and they hung me up so high
and I'll piss right in their eye, fuck them all.

oh, my name is knobby hall, knobby hall...
and I've only got one ball,
but tis better than none at all, fuck them all

Oh, the parson he will come, he will come...
with his tales of kingdom come

he can shove them up his bum, fuck them all

Oh. the sheriff will come too, will come too...
with his mother fucking crew
they've got fuck all else to do, fuck them all

Oh, my name is knobby hall, knobby hall...
and I've only got one ball
but tis better than none at all, fuck them all

I see molly in the crowd, in the crowd...
and I feel so goddamn proud
that I want to shout out loud, fuck them all
oh, my name is knobby hall, knobby hall...
but tis better than none at all, fuck them all

2, Albert *Hall.*

The Royal Albert Hall was originally going to be called the Central Hall.

It was built in the heart of the South Kensington estate, to fulfil the vision of Prince Albert in promoting appreciation of the Arts and Sciences.

When Prince Albert died of typhoid fever in 1861, the plans were put on hold until rekindled by Albert's collaborator on the Great Exhibition, Henry Cole.

Work started in April 1867 and the Hall was opened on 29 March 1871 by Queen Victoria, renamed in Prince Albert's memory ao the 'Royal Albert Hall of Arts and Sciences'.

HARE

Jack has always loved sports personalities, Dusty Hare is one...

Dusty *Hare.*

William Henry "Dusty" Hare, a former international England rugby union footballer, who played fullback who was born in Newark-on-Trent.

Hare currently, (*at time of writing*), holds the world record for points scored in a first-class rugby career with 7,337 points.

Hare played for Newark RUFC & Nottingham R.F.C. before joining Leicester Tigers and playing nearly 400 games for them.

He made his England debut 16 March 1974 in a match against Wales, and played his final game ten years later, having gained 25 caps. He toured with the British Lions to New Zealand in 1983.

He retired from club rugby after the 1989 cup final loss to Bath

HEART

Ticker *Heart.*

Play on someone's heart beating, or "ticking".

HARRIS

Whatever service the prominent figures came from, Jack was always happy to bequeath their names to his oppos.

1, Bomber *Harris.*

After WW2 Head of Bomber Command, Air Chief Sir Arthur Harris.

Marshal of the Royal Air Force, Sir Arthur Travers Harris, 1st Baronet, GCB, OBE, AFC, commonly known as "Bomber" Harris by the press (*and often, within the RAF as "Butcher" Harris,*) was Air Officer Commanding-in-Chief (AOC-in-C) RAF Bomber Command during the strategic bombing campaign against Nazi Germany in the Second World War.

When 17 years old, in 1910, Harris emigrated to Southern Rhodesia but returned to England in 1915 to fight in the First World War.

He joined the Royal Flying Corps, which became the Royal Air Force in 1918. Harris served through the 1920s and 1930s, in India, Mesopotamia, Persia, Egypt, Palestine.

At the outbreak of the Second World War, He took command of No. 5 Group RAF in England. In February 1942 was appointed head of Bomber Command. A position he kept for the rest of the war.

After the war, Harris moved to South Africa where he managed the South African Marine Corporation.

2, Chats *Harris*

It is unclear of how the name 'Chats' became associated with Harris, but as with many words the original meaning of 'chats/chatts' has changed over time.

It has included the female pudenda, a hole in the wall convicts used to communicate, even a word meaning to search for head lice.

However, the most likely connection associated with the Royal Navy is the name for seaman from Medway.

Sailors from Chatham docks and depot were known locally as 'Chatham Rats'. This was often shortened to 'Chats'.

Who, or what, the 'Harris' connection may be is unfortunately lost in unrecorded history.

(*Unless you know otherwise?*)

3, Chopper *Harris*

Ronald Harris was a footballer for Chelsea where he played as a fullback in the 1960's and '70's.

He was given the nickname 'Chopper' due to his hard tackling. Chopper is regarded as one of the toughest defenders of his era, along with Tommy Smith and Norman Hunter.

4, Wiggy *Harris*

Harrison Harry Max Harrison, often called 'Wiggy', (*for ease, no doubt*), was an American science fiction author, known for his character the Stainless-Steel Rat and for his novel 'Make Room! Make Room was the rough basis for the movie 'Soylent Green'.

HAYCOCK

Strawballs *Haycock*

This one needs no explanation.

HAYES

Yep, Jack loves watching a true blue Wessy...

Gabby *Hayes*

George Francis "Gabby" Hayes, best known for his appearances in Western films as a sidekick of the leading man.

Hayes was cast as a partner of the Western stars Randolph Scott (six times) and John Wayne (15 times, sometimes as villainous character).

Hayes played Wayne's sidekick in Raoul Walsh's Dark Command (1940), which featured Roy Rogers in a supporting role.

HENDERSON

This is an amazing and touching true story which made the worlds media and was picked up by Jack.

Granny *Henderson*

America 1976.

The National Park Service classified Buffalo National River and the surrounding 95,000 acres a protected area.

Land Acquisition officers visited Eva Barnes Henderson, known to everyone as "Granny."

Granny Henderson lived in a four-room cabin in Buffalo Valley, on 160 acres of land she and her husband farmed since 1912.

Granny told the Park Service agents she wouldn't sell her home *"for anything."*

She was informed (*told*) her home would be condemned and the land taken if she did not leave willingly.

After several years of pressure, Granny finally agreed and her family built her a new home.

It was wintertime and Granny asked the Park Service for an extension of time before she moved. Wanting to wait until the weather warmed up.

The Park Service agreed but made her pay rent on the land she lived on for 65 years.

For Granny, the thing of all was having to give up her beloved livestock, for who she'd carried water to & from her well every day, for over half a century.

On the day of the move, Granny begged to stay in her cabin until the last of her possessions were hauled away.

She sat on a stool and cried all day.

Granny's health deteriorated rapidly and she moved in with her family who took care of her.

She died in 1979, three years after the National Park Service first knocked on her cabin door.

Granny only spent two days in her new house.

HEWITT

We regularly associate the word 'nosh' with food. Here's why.

Nosher *Hewitt*

The word, '*Nosher*', is first recorded in the Early 20th century.

Its origination is probably an amalgamation of the Yiddish 'Nasher', (*from the Middle High German word Nasher/Nascher/ Näscher*) meaning a person with a sweet tooth and from Neschen/Naschen referring to eat dainty foods or delicacies, often abbreviated to 'Nosh'.

How this word has become synonymous with the surname Hewitt is unclear. But you can imagine someone digging into their scran like a starving shitehawk...

HIGGIN(S)

Henry *Higgins*

Henry Higgins, a fictional character in George Bernard Shaw's play, Pygmalion (1913).

In 1938, a film version was called 'My Fair Lady', in which Leslie Howard played Henry Higgins, a professor of phonetics who bets he can teach Cockney flower girl Eliza Doolittle to speak 'proper' English.

This was adapted for theatre in 1964, with Rex Harrison playing the professor.

HILL

1, Bunker *Hill*

On June 17, 1775, early in the American War of Independence, (1775-83), the British defeated the Americans at Bunker Hill in Massachusetts, which was part of a greater battle, known as the Siege of Boston

The battle is named after Bunker Hill, which was the original objective of both the colonial and British troops, though most of the combat took place on the adjacent hill which later became known as Breed's Hill.

This one is pure Navy

1, Pusser *Hill*

On Tortola in the British Virgin Islands, you will find the headquarters of a three-hundred-year-old business many may be familiar with... Pusser's Rum Ltd.

Pusser's produce this fine Grog in five distilleries, located in Guyana and Trinidad. These distilleries are all set 'up a hill', well above sea level which offers some protection from the sea during tropical storms.

You could say they were on 'Pusser Hill'

2, Hence, Upper *Hill*

3, and Windy *Hill*

These need no explanation.

HINDS

Cosher *Hinds*

As I have previously stated, language is not static. The use of words alters over generations, many are lost to academic archives, others take on new meanings.

Cosher is one such word.

In British languages, it is a derivative of Coisir, an Irish word dating back to the 1630's meaning Feast/Entertainment.

Other uses for Cosher are 'to sponge' off another, living at someone else's expense, but it is also used to mean 'to visit' & have a friendly talk/chat and to show/hold a 'fondness', to excessively 'dote' on another.

In more recent times Cosher has been confused with, (*and its meaning often replaced*), by the phonetically same sounding word 'Kosher'.

However, I can find no records of its adoption to the name of Hinds, or any accredited application regarding the Royal Navy.

Another of Jacks mysteries we may never solve.

HOGAN

1, Ben *Hogan*

William Ben Hogan 1912 – 1997, was an American professional golfer considered one of the greatest players in the history.

Hogan is noted for his influence on golf swing theory and his legendary ball-striking ability.

His nine career professional major championships tie him with Gary Player for fourth all-time, trailing only Jack Nicklaus (18), Tiger Woods (14) and Walter Hagen (11).

He is one of only five golfers who won all four major championships open to professionals (the Master's Tournament, The Open (*despite only playing once*), the U.S. Open, and the PGA Championship).

2, Hec(k) *Hogan*

Hector "Hec" Denis Hogan, an Australian athlete who competed in the 100 yards and 100 metres sprint.

He was seven-times Australian 100 yards champion.

He competed in the 220 yards/200 metres, which he won twice in the Australian Championships, and in the long jump which he won in 1954.

In March 1954, he equalled the world record for the 100 yards (9.3 seconds) and 100 metres (10.2 seconds) on a grass track in Sydney.

Hec(k) competed for Australia in the 1956 Summer Olympics in Melbourne. He won the bronze medal in the 100 metres.

3, Hulk *Hogan.*

A more recent nickname, Hulk Hogan, is a retired professional wrestler. His real name is Terry Gene Bollea.

Hogan is regarded as the greatest professional wrestler of all time.

Hogan's acting career began with Rocky III. He starred in several movies (including No Holds Barred, Suburban Commando and Mr. Nanny) along with three television shows (Thunder in Paradise, Hogan Knows Best and China, IL).

You may have also seen him in Right Guard antiperspirant adverts or in the video game, Hulk Hogan's Main Event.

HOLLAND

Dutch(y) *Holland*

A simple play on words.

HOLDING

Scaff *Holding*

Another play on words.

HOLMES

1, Sherlock *Holmes*

Sherlock Holmes, a fictional private detective created by the author Sir Arthur Conan Doyle.

First appearing in print in 1887, in A Study in Scarlet, the character's popularity became widespread with the first series of short stories in The Strand Magazine, beginning with "A Scandal in Bohemia" in 1891.

Though not the first fictional detective, Sherlock Holmes is arguably the best known, with Guinness World Records listing him as the "most portrayed movie character" in history.

The character and stories have a profound effect on mystery writing with the original tales, along with those written by other authors, being adapted for the stage, radio, television, films and even video games.

2, Noshit *Sherlock*

Need I explain this one... I think not.

HONEYBUN(N)

Gus *Honeybun*

Gus Honeybun, A puppet rabbit and the station mascot for Westward Television and Television South West, from 1961 to 1992.

Honeybun was given the full name of Augustus Jeremiah Honeybun by a continuity announcer. The puppet was devised to fill unsold advertising slots during children's TV broadcasts.

Gus appeared with many television personalities, including Ian Stirling, Fern Britton, Judi Spiers, David Fitzgerald, Ruth Langsford & Sally Meen.

HORN

Some people seem to lead extraordinary lives...

1, Trader *Horn*

Alfred Aloysius "Trader" Horn, born Alfred Aloysius Smith in 1861, was an ivory trader in central Africa.

He wrote a book, *Trader Horn: A Young Man's Astounding Adventures in 19th-Century Equatorial Africa,* detailing his journeys into jungles teeming with buffalo, gorillas, man-eating leopards, serpents and "savages".

The book documents Trader's efforts to free slaves, meet the founder of Rhodesia, Cecil Rhodes and liberate a princess from captivity.

Trader Horn became the subject of several films. There was also a 1973 remake of the 1931 film simply called 'Trader Horn'. The film is based on Traders own book and tells of the adventures he experienced whilst on safari in Africa.

A nice old salty sailors name...

2, Cape *Horn*

Cape Horn is a rocky headland on Hornos Island, in southern Chile's Tierra del Fuego archipelago. It is often surrounded by wild seas where the Pacific and Atlantic oceans meet.

Cape Horn is the most southerly point of mainland South America.

The albatross-shaped Cape Horn Monument commemorates the lives of thousands of seafarers who perished attempting to sail around the cape.

A secluded lighthouse and the tiny Stella-Maris Chapel are nearby.

Cape Horn was deemed to be the halfway point from England to Australia during the nineteenth-century clipper route.

HORNER

Jack *Horner*

The earliest reference to the verse is in *Namby Pamby*, a ballad by Henry Carey published in 1725. It suggests this rhyme was known by the early eighteenth century

The rhyme is often said to be about Thomas Horner, steward to Richard Whiting, the last abbot of Glastonbury before the dissolution of the monasteries under Henry VIII of England.

It is reported, prior to the abbey's destruction, the abbot sent Horner to London with a huge Christmas pie, containing the deeds to a dozen or more manorial lands, hidden within its clacker coating. Some say it was sent as a gift, others a bribe, to convince the King not to nationalize Church lands.

The story goes... during his journey to London, Horner opened the pie, taking the deeds of the manor of Mells in Somerset for himself.

The Mells Manor's properties included lead mines of the Mendip Hills, causing speculation the word 'plumb' is a literary pun on the Latin word plumbum, meaning lead.

Little Jack Horner
Sat in the corner,
Eating his Christmas pie;
He put in his thumb,
And pulled out a plum,
And said, "What a good boy am I

HOWE

Gibley *Howe*

I have been able to find little information regarding this name pairing.

However, I did find the following suggestion regarding 'Gibley', which I found extremely funny and very relatable.

Knowing Jack's humour, this is probably the closest and best guess, without written proof for the names pairing.

"Someone who uses dried cat turds for breath mints spends all their time hanging over your shoulder making moronic comments."

"Have you ever met a bigger idiot than Howe? he is a real Gibley".

HUBBARD

Mother *Hubbard*

Old Mother Hubbard is an English nursery rhyme, first printed in 1805 and among the most popular of the nineteenth century.

The exact origin and meaning of the rhyme is disputed. The first published version, by Sarah Catherine Martin, while staying in a 400-year-old stone cottage in Yealmpton. (pronounced "yamt'n"), a village in Devon.

The lyrics originally published in 1805 have remained largely unchanged.

Old Mother Hubbard
Went to the cupboard,
To give the poor dog a bone;
But when she came there
The cupboard was bare,
And so, the poor dog had none.

She went to the baker's

To buy him some bread;

When she came back

The dog was dead!

She went to the undertaker's

To buy him a coffin;

When she came back

The dog was laughing.

She took a clean dish

to get him some tripe;

When she came back

He was smoking his pipe.

She went to the alehouse

To get him some beer;

When she came back

The dog sat in a chair.

She went to the tavern

For white wine and red;

When she came back

The dog stood on his head.

She went to the fruiterer's

To buy him some fruit;

When she came back

He was playing the flute.

She went to the tailor's

To buy him a coat;

When she came back

He was riding a goat.

She went to the hatter's

To buy him a hat;

When she came back

He was feeding her cat.

She went to the barber's

To buy him a wig

When she came back

He was dancing a jig.

She went to the cobbler's

To buy him some shoes;

When she came back

He was reading the news.

She went to the sempstress
To buy him some linen;
When she came back
The dog was spinning.

She went to the hosier's
To buy him some hose;
When she came back
He was dressed in his clothes.

The Dame made a curtsy,
The dog made a bow;
The Dame said, Your servant;
The dog said, Bow-wow.

This wonderful dog
Was Dame Hubbard's delight,
He could read, he could dance,
He could sing, he could write;

She gave him rich dainties

Whenever he fed,

And erected this monument

When he was dead.

HUDSON

1, Rock *Hudson*

Rock Hudson, Roy Harold Scherer Jr, an American actor known for playing the leading man in many films during the 1950s and 1960s. He was a 'heartthrob' of the Hollywood 'Golden Age'.

Rock appeared in nearly 70 films and starred in several television productions during a career spanning over four decades. In 1956 he was nominated for an Oscar for his role in Giant.

2, Soapy *Hudson*

Taken from A brand of soap issued to the Royal Naval Fleet, produced by a company called Hudson.

Robert Spear Hudson was born in West Bromwich.

In 1937 Hudson began making soap powder in the rear of his shop by grinding course soap bars with a pestle and mortar.

Before this people needed to make soap flakes themselves. Hudson's soap flakes became the first commercially viable soap 'powder'.

Hudson sold his business to Lever Brothers, as a subsidiary enterprise, in 1908. They retained the Hudson name until around the early 1930's when the brand names of Rinso and Omo were introduced.

The company, R. S. Hudson and Co continued as a subsidiary within the Unilever empire for several years after WWII.

HUGHES

1, Flapper *Hughes*

No, this name is not from someone panicking, nor is it a term for a female's nether regions, as some might have you believe.

It is probably after the actress of the 1920's, Leonore Hughes.

She was born in Chicago in 1897, known for The Rejected Woman (1924) and The Indestructible Wife (1919).

'Flappers' were a generation of fashionable young women during this era. They wore short skirts, bobbed hair, listened to jazz and flaunted their disdain for what was considered acceptable behaviour.

Flappers played on being brash, wearing excessive makeup, drinking alcohol, smoking cigars and tobacco, treating sex in a casual manner, driving cars and flouting social and sexual norms.

2, Spike *Hughes*

Patrick Cairns "Spike" Hughes, the son of Irish composer, writer and song collector Herbert Hughes and great-grandson of the sculptor Samuel Peploe Wood, was a British jazz musician (bass), composer and bandleader during the 1930's & 40's.

He was a multi-dimensional musician, playing the double bass, composing operatic scores, arranging jazz recordings and writing books on topics ranging from gardening to Toscanini's music.

HUNT

1, Whatuk *Hunt*

I'll say no more about this.

2, PeeWee *Hunt*

Born with the name of Walter Gerhardt Hunt, Pee Wee was a jazz trombonist, vocalist and bandleader.

He was the co-founder of the Casa Loma Orchestra, but in 1943 to work as a Hollywood radio disc jockey before joining the Merchant Marine near the end of World War II.

His "Twelfth Street Rag" was a three million-selling number one hit in September 1948.

He was satirized as Pee Wee Runt and his All-Flea Dixieland Band in Tex Avery's animated MGM cartoon Dixieland Droopy (1954).

His second major hit was "Oh" (1953), his second million-selling disc, which reached number three in the Billboard chart.

*I'm guessing Jack took the name from the Micky-duck, Droopy cartoon rather than the hit music… but I'll leave you to decide which you think is more **RN** (ish).*

I & J

India & Juliet

Amazingly there are no records or anecdotal chronicles regarding the letter 'I' in Royal Naval archives on nicknames.

If you have any substantiated and supported information on any missing 'I', I would like to know.

Thank you.

JACK

Dusty *Jack*

Traditional nickname for a junior member of the victualling staff, also known as "Dusty-boy".

The term has its origin in the early 1800s when ship's stewards were known as "Jack-in-the-dust", referring to the dusty atmosphere created by issuing quantities of flour and dried biscuit and whose responsibility included doling out the daily tot of rum to sailors and maintaining the ship's inventory of food supplies.

JAMES

1, Jimmy *James*

He was a music hall, film, radio and television comedian and comedy actor. James had limited use for jokes, preferring to say things in a humorous manner, sometimes in surreal situations and as such was seen by some as ahead of his time. We now refer to this form as 'Observational comedy'.

Jimmy was often hailed as a "comedian's' comedian".

2, Latterly, the term may refer to Michael "Jimmy" James, a Jamaican soul singer known for his songs "Come to Me Softly", "Now Is the Time" and "I'll Go Where the Music Takes Me".

Based in Britain, James has performed as the lead singer of Jimmy James and the Vagabonds since the mid-1960s.

3, Jessie *James*

Another true-blue western, but a true tale this time.

Jesse Woodson James, American outlaw, bank and train robber and leader of the James–Younger Gang.

Raised in the "Little Dixie" area of western Missouri.

He and his brother, Frank James, joined pro-Confederate guerrillas known as "bushwhackers" operating in Missouri and Kansas during the American Civil War.

As followers of William Quantrill and "Bloody Bill" Anderson, they were accused of participating in atrocities against Union soldiers and civilian abolitionists, including the Centralia Massacre in 1864.

After the war, as members of various gangs of outlaws, Jesse and Frank robbed banks, stagecoaches and trains across Midwest America, gaining national fame and popular sympathy despite the brutality of their crimes.

On April 3, 1882, Jesse James was shot and killed by Robert Ford, a recruit to the gang, who hoped to collect a reward on James' head. Already a celebrity in life, James became a legendary figure of the Wild West after his death.

JONES

1, Spike *Jones*

Perhaps after Lindley Armstrong Jones, known as Spike Jones, who was born 1911 in Long Beach, California.

He received his nickname "Spike" from his father's employment at the Southern Pacific Railroad.

In high school, Jones learnt the drums and went on to a distinguished career in the band The City Slickers which performed parodies of popular songs in the 1940s to the mid-1950s.

2, Casey *Jones*

Most probably after, Jonathan Luther "Casey" Jones from Jackson, Tennessee.

He was an American railroader who worked for the Illinois Central Railroad (IC).

Casey was killed on April 30, 1900, when his train collided with a stalled freight train near Vaughan, Mississippi. His dramatic death while trying to stop his train and save the lives of his passengers made him a hero.

Casey Jones was immortalised in a popular ballad by his friend Wallace Saunders, an engine wiper for the IC.

Come, all you rounders, if you want to hear
The story told of a brave engineer;
Casey Jones was the rounder's name
A high right-wheeler of mighty fame."
Of mighty fame, of mighty fame
A high right-wheeler of mighty fame
Casey pulled into the Memphis yard
Fed up, beat down and dog tired
Another driver had called in sick
Asking Casey to do a double trick
Casey smiled, said, "I'm feelin' fine
Gonna ride that train to the end of the line
There's ridges and bridges, and hills to climb
Got a head of steam and ahead of time."
Ahead of time, ahead of time
Got a head of steam and ahead of time

Caller called Casey, half-past four;

He kissed his wife, the station door

Climbed into the cab, orders in his hand

"Could be my trip to the Promised Land."

Through South Memphis on the fly

The fireman say, "You got a white eye."

The switchmen knew the engine's moan

The man at the throttle was Casey Jones

Was Casey Jones, was Casey Jones

The man at the throttle was Casey Jones

The engine rocked, the drivers rolled

Fireman hollered, "Save my soul!"

"I'm gonna roll her 'til she leaves the rails

I'm behind time with the Southern mail

Been raining hard for weeks and weeks;

Railroad track like the bed of a creek

Rated down to a thirty-mile gait ---

The Southern mail two hours late

Two hours late, two hours late

The Southern mail was two hours late

Fireman say, "You running too fast

You ran the last three lights we passed

Casey say, "We'll make it through

She's steamin' better than I ever knew."

Casey say, "Don't you fret

Keep feedin' the fire; don't give up yet

Run her 'til she leaves the rail

To be on time with the Southern mail

The Southern Mail, the Southern mail

To be on time with the Southern mail

Checked his water, his water was low

Looked at his watch, his watch was slow

Put on more water, put on more coal

Put your head out the window see my drivers roll

See my drivers roll, see my drivers roll

Put your head out the window see my drivers roll

People said Casey couldn't run

But I can tell you what Casey done;

Left Memphis, quarter 'til nine

Vaughn, Mississippi, right on time

Got within a mile of the place

A big headlight stared him in the face;

Shout to the fireman, "Jump for your life."

Give my love to my children, say goodbye to my wife

Casey said, just before he died

"There's a lot more railroads that I'd like to ride;"

He said the good Lord whispered, "It'll never be,"

The Illinois Central be the death of me

Headaches and heartaches and all kinds of pain

Ain't no different from a railroad train

You can take your stories, noble and grand

All just a part of a railroad man.....

K

KILO

KAIN/KANE (Cain/Cane)

Another great military true tale.

Cobber *Kain*

After Edgar James Kain, DFC.

Kain was a New Zealand fighter pilot flying ace who flew in the Royal Air Force (RAF) during the Second World War.

Known to others as 'Killer Kain'. Edgar was affectionately known as 'Cobber' by his RAF colleagues due to his antipodean heritage.

He completed his flight training in 1937, joined No.73 Squadron, flew the Gloucester Gladiator and the Hawker Hurricane.

At the outbreak of the Second World War, he went to France as part of the Advanced Air Striking Force (AASF).

Kain began flying operational sorties during the Phoney War and gained his first victory in November 1939.

A second followed days later. In March he claimed his fifth victory becoming the first fighter ace (*a pilot credited with five or more enemy aircraft destroyed in aerial combat*) and the first recipient of the Distinguished Flying Cross during WWII.

During these encounters, his plane was damaged on occasion and he was wounded.

The Phoney War ended on 10 May 1940 when the Battle of France and the Low Countries began. Within 17 days, Kain claimed a further 12 aerial victories. His success so early in the war saw him become a household name in Britain.

Deemed to be physically exhausted Kain was ordered to return home on 7 June 1940. Having bid farewell to his squadron, in a gesture to his comrades, he took off in a Hurricane to perform a series of low-level aerobatics over Échemines airfield.

Kain crashed at high speed and was killed instantly. At the time of his death, he held the rank of flying officer and was credited with 17 aerial victories against the Luftwaffe.

KAY/KAYE

Danny Kay

Danny Kaye an American actor, singer, dancer, comedian and musician. His performances featured physical comedy, idiosyncratic pantomimes and rapid-fire novelty songs.

Kaye starred in 17 movies. His films were popular, especially his performances of patter songs and favourites such as "Inchworm" and "The Ugly Duckling."

He was the first ambassador-at-large of UNICEF in 1954 and received the French Legion of Honour in 1986 for his years of work with the organisation.

KELLY

1, Ned *Kelly*

Edward Kelly an Australian outlaw, gang leader and convicted police murderer. One of the last bushrangers and the most famous, he is known for wearing bulletproof armour during his final shootout with the police.

Kelly was born in the British colony of Victoria as the third of eight children to Irish parents. His father, a transported convict, died shortly after serving a six-month prison sentence, leaving Kelly, then aged 12, as the eldest male of the household.

While a teenager he was arrested for associating with bushranger Harry Power and served two prison terms for a variety of offences, the longest stretch being from 1871 to 1874 on a conviction of receiving a stolen horse. Kelly would later join the "Greta mob", a group of bush larrikins known for stock theft.

Kelly and his gang eluded the police for two years with the support of an extensive network of sympathisers. The gang's crime spree included armed bank robberies at Euroa and Jerilderie and the killing of Aaron Sherritt, a sympathiser turned police informer.

In 1880, when Kelly's attempt to derail and ambush a police train failed, he and his gang, dressed in armour fashioned from stolen plough mouldboards, engaged in a final gun battle with the police at Glenrowan.

Kelly, the only survivor, was severely wounded by police fire and captured. Despite thousands of supporters attending rallies and signing a petition for his reprieve, Kelly was tried, convicted and sentenced to death by hanging, which was carried out at the Old Melbourne Gaol. His last words were famously reported to have been, "such is life".

Martin Flanagan wrote:

"What makes Ned a legend is not that everyone sees him the same. It's that everyone sees him. Like a bushfire on the horizon casting its red glow into the night."

2, Spider *Kelly*

Nicknames of Jim Kelly, featherweight boxing champion (1938-39) and his son Billy Kelly champion at the same weight (1955-56).

He was the first professional Irish boxer to hold the same titles as his father. He won both the British and Empire featherweight championships, as his father Jimmy "Spider Kelly" had in the 1930s.

Kelly was born in 1932 on the Lecky Road in Derry's Bogside, the eldest of 10 children to James "Spider" Kelly. He inherited the nickname Spider from his father, along with the love of boxing. As an amateur, he won two Ulster juvenile titles and at 18, moved to England and turned professional.

Eamonn McCann remembers the excitement:

"He was the great hero at a time when there was nothing much to rejoice about. He was the person everybody hitched their hopes to. His fights were followed on the radio and are embedded in the consciousness of an older generation."

KERR

1, Wayne *Kerr*

Just say it quickly and listen.

2, Peggy *Kerr*

No idea whatsoever.

3, Con *Kerr*

Never knew if this was 'Conker' or 'Concur'.

Do you know?

KIRBY

Rip *Kirby*

Rip Kirby is a comic strip featuring the adventures of the eponymous lead character, a private detective created by Alex Raymond in 1946.

After World War II, Raymond did not return to work on any of his previous successful comic strips *(Flash Gordon, Jungle Jim, Secret Agent X-9)* but began work on a new strip in which ex-Marine Rip Kirby returns from World War II and goes to work as a private detective, sometimes accompanied by his girlfriend, fashion model Judith Lynne "Honey" Dorian.

The strip enjoyed success, and Raymond received the Reuben Award in 1949

KING

Jason *King*

Jason King is a British television series starring Peter Wyngarde as the titular character.

It was produced by ITC Entertainment for a season of 26 one-hour long episodes.

It was shown internationally as well as in the UK and has been released on DVD in the UK, US, Australia and Germany.

Subsequent episodes featured Wyngarde playing King trying to write his novels and being pressured by his publisher Nicola Harvester about deadlines.

King, however, was usually distracted by beautiful women and his real-life adventures and was sometimes tricked by Ryland of the British Government into assisting the Government in international political matters: all of which later found their way into the adventures of the fictional Mark Caine.

KNIGHT

1, Barry/Barrie *Knight* &/or **2,** Bogey *Knight*

Both nicknames are of the same origin.

Barrie 'Bogey' Knight was involved in most conflicts the Royal Marines participated in after the Second World War.

Joining in 1958, Bogey went to Malaya, Borneo, the Persian Gulf, Aden, Northern Ireland and the Falklands.

He was Sergeant Major aboard HMS Fearless during the Falklands War.

His responsibilities included the care of survivors from HMS Antelope, Sir Tristram and Sir Galahad, the resupply of weapons, kit and ammunition.

Those aboard Fearless deployed to the Falklands via Landing Craft.

He was the last Sergeant Major to ring the bell in the Sergeant's Mess at Eastney when the barracks closed in 1991. He retired in 1993, as Corps Property Warrant Officer.

2, From the "*Colonel Bogey March*", a march composed in 1914 by Lieutenant F. J. Ricketts (1881–1945) (pen name Kenneth J. Alford), a British Army bandmaster who later became the director of music for the Royal Marines at Plymouth.

L

Lima

LAMB

Larry *Lamb*

Probably?

1, Larry the Lamb was created by Sydney George Hulme Beaman as one of a series of carved wooden figures for 'Toytown', a series of books beginning with 'The Road to Toytown', in 1925.

The books were adapted to radio in 1929, where the stuttering character of Larry the Lamb and his best friend, Dennis the Dachshund, became listeners favourites as their misadventures caused bewilderment to the other Toytown residents.

2, Possibly?

Larry Lamb, British TV actor known for role in the 1970's BBC soap series "Triangle".

Lawrence Douglas Lamb played Archie Mitchell in the BBC soap opera EastEnders, Mick Shipman in the BBC romantic comedy series Gavin & Stacey and Ted Case in the final series of the BBC Crime Drama New Tricks. He was also on I'm A Celebrity Get Me Out of Here 2016.

LANE

1, Shady *Lane*

Play on lanes being shady places.

2, Lois *Lane*

Comic book character.

In the early comic books, Lois Lane's parents were farmers in a town called Pittsdale.

She is the daughter of Sam Lane and his wife Ella Lane.

In the modern comics, Lois's father Sam Lane is a military officer and Lois is a former army brat, with Lois having been trained by her father in areas such as hand-to-hand combat and the use of firearms.

Lois was created by writer Jerry Siegel and artist Joe Shuster, her first appearance was in Action Comics No.1, released in June 1938.

She is designed as a counterpart and the love interest to Superman and his alter ego Clark Kent.

Her appearance and personality were based on various people. Lois's original physical appearance was based on Joanne Carter.

LARKIN, LARKING

1, Sky *Larkin*

Play on skylarking

2, Pop *Larkin*

Taken from the television series, 'The Darling Buds of May', first shown 7 April 1991 until the 4 April 1993.

The character Sidney 'Pop' Larkin was played by the actor David Jason

LAWTON

Tommy *Lawton*

Thomas Lawton was an English football player and manager. A strong centre-forward with excellent all-around attacking skills, he was able to head with the ball with tremendous power and accuracy.

Born in Farnworth (6 October 1919 – 6 November 1996) he turned professional at Burnley on his 17th birthday.

He also played cricket for Burnley Cricket Club, before his potential as a footballer won him a £6,500 move to Everton in January 1937. He went on to finish as the First Division's top-scorer in 1938 and 1939, helping Everton to finish as champions of the Football League in the latter campaign.

In November 1947, he made a surprise move to Third Division South club Notts County for a British record transfer fee of £20,000. He helped the club to win promotion as champions in 1949–50'

He scored 22 goals in his 23 England appearances over a ten-year international career from 1938 to 1948, including four against Portugal in May 1947. He helped England to win two British Home Championship titles outright (1946–47 and 1947–48), and to share the Championship in 1938–39.

LEACH, LEECH

Buck *Leach*

No data regarding this name association.

LEE, LEIGH

1, Dixie *Lee*

Dixie Lee, the American actress, dancer and singer was the first wife of singer Bing Crosby. Born Wilma Winifred Wyatt in Harriman, Tennessee on November 4, 1911.

2, Tansy *Lee*

Tansy is a corruption of Tancy *Lee,* a Scottish boxer at flyweight, bantamweight and featherweight. He was the first Scot to win a British title and became the European and World champion.

Lee had his first fights as an amateur in 1906.

Undefeated as a professional by 1911, he suffered his first loss, (by stoppage), in the thirteenth round against Alex Lafferty in a contest for the Scottish bantamweight title.

Tancy won the Scottish flyweight title three years later when he beat Dan McGrady.

After retiring from the ring Lee became a bookmaker and a boxing trainer/manager. He co-founded the Leith Victoria Club in 1919 and trained Johnny Hill, Alex Ireland, Jim Rolland and Lee's nephews, George McKenzie and James McKenzie, both Olympic medallists. George also won the British featherweight title.

Tancy Lee died on 5 February 1941, aged 59, after being hit by a bus in Duncan Place, and was buried at Seafield Cemetery in Edinburgh.

Lee was inducted into the Scottish Boxing Hall of Fame in September 2008, in a ceremony attended by his 94-year-old daughter.

LEWIS

Jerry *Lewis*

Jerry Lewis was born on March 16, 1926, as either Jerome Levitch or Joseph Levitch, depending on the source you believe.

He was an American comedian, actor, singer, director, producer, screenwriter, humanitarian and headliner. He was known for his slapstick humour in film, television, stage and radio and was nicknamed the "King of Comedy".

LITTLE

Tiny *Little*

Surely no explanation needed here.

LIVINGSTONE

Doc *Livingstone*

David Livingstone, a Scottish Christian Congregationalist, a pioneer medical missionary with the London Missionary Society, an explorer in Africa and one of the most popular British heroes of the late-19th-century in the Victorian era.

His main fame is as a traveller with an obsession for reaching the sources of the Nile River.

His meeting with Henry Morton Stanley on 10 November 1871 gave rise to the popular, but anachronistic, quotation

"Dr Livingstone, I presume?"

LLOYD

Larry *Lloyd*

Laurence Valentine Lloyd, a retired association football central defender and manager was a 1970s central defender for Liverpool and Nottingham Forest football clubs, with whom he won 2 European Cup winners' medals.

He won domestic and European honours for both Bill Shankly's Liverpool and Brian Clough's Nottingham Forest in the 1970s.

LONDON

Smokey *London*

The City of London is known as "the Smoke".

The nickname for the city came from the low-grade post-war coal, burned primarily in homes, which caused an increased amount of sulphur dioxide, polluting the foggy air, giving the common term 'Smog'.

Additional contributions to the smog were from the abundant coal-fired power stations in the Greater London area, including Fulham, Battersea, Bankside and Kingston upon Thames, all of which added to the air's contamination.

Pea soup, or a Pea Souper, otherwise known as a black fog or killer fog, is very thick and has a yellowish green hue. Black smog is caused by soot and the noxious gas sulphur dioxide.

LONG

Dodger *Long*

Play on words

LOWE

Arthur *Lowe*

Arthur Lowe's career spanned over thirty years, including theatre and television productions. He is best known for playing Captain Mainwaring in Dad's Army.

He was nominated for seven BAFTAs and became one of the most recognised faces on television.

It was not until he played 'Leonard Swindley' in Coronation Street that he became a household name. He played the character until 1966.

In 1968 he took his role in Dad's Army. The success of this character led to considerable television and theatrical work, which put pressure on his health.

Lowe's final years were dominated by alcoholism and illness and he died from a stroke on 15 April 1982, aged 66.

M

MIKE

MARSH

Swampy *Marsh*

Play on words – in the sense of boggy ground

MARSHALL

Scrumpy *Marshall*

The Marshall general purpose engine (Tractor), circa 1906 - 1927 was named ' Scrumpy'.

Possibly used during the apple harvest to haul the produce from the orchards to the cider presses.

MARTIN

1, Pincher *Martin*

Admiral Sir William Fanshawe Martin, son of Admiral Sir Thomas Byam Martin, learnt his trade as a midshipman under William Bligh and served as a lieutenant on Victory under Nelson in 1804.

Sir William was a keen disciplinarian and is the original 'Pincher' Martin, so-called because he would have men 'pinched' (arrested), for the most minor of offences.

When Martin arrived in the Mediterranean he found the fleet in a state of unrest.

"By tact, by care, by unremitting attention and by judicious severity" Pincher Martin brought it into admirable order.

(According to legend).

It is said he would hoist "Bury your dead" as a matter of routine upon the completion of Monday seamanship evolutions.

Admiral W F Martin was the 4th Baronet, GCB (5 December 1801 – 24 March 1895), a commander, provided valuable support to British merchants at Callao in Peru in the early 1820s during the Peruvian War of Independence.

He became First Naval Lord in the Second Derby–Disraeli ministry in March 1858 and in that capacity acted as a strong advocate for the procurement of Britain's first ironclad warship.

Pincher became Commander-in-Chief, Mediterranean Fleet and provided assistance during the Italian disturbances.

In 1860 and 1861, he reformed the system of discipline in his fleet and developed a comprehensive system of manoeuvres for steamships.

2, Pincher *Martin*

Pincher Martin (*published in America as Pincher Martin: The Two Deaths of Christopher Martin*), is a novel by British writer William Golding, first published in 1956. It was Golding's third novel, following 'The Inheritors' and 'Lord of the Flies'.

The plot of Pincher Martin surrounds the survival and psychophysical, spiritual and existential plight of one Christopher Hadley "Pincher" Martin, a temporary naval lieutenant who believes himself to be the sole survivor of a military torpedo destroyer which sinks in the North Atlantic Ocean.

MASON

Perry *Mason*

Perry Mason is an American legal drama broadcast on CBS television from September 21, 1957, to May 22, 1966.

The title character, portrayed by Raymond Burr, is a Los Angeles criminal defence lawyer, (who originally appeared in detective fiction by Erle Stanley Gardner).

The New Perry Mason, a 1973 revival of the series with a different cast, was poorly received and only ran for 15 episodes.

In 1985, a successful series of 30 Perry Mason television films aired on NBC, with Burr reprising the role of Mason in 26 of them before his death in 1993.

MATTHEWS

Stanley (Stan) *Matthews*

Often regarded as one of the greatest players of the British game, Sir Stanley Matthews is the only player to be knighted while still playing football,

He is the first winner of both the European Footballer of the Year and the Football Writers' Association Footballer of the Year awards. Matthews' nicknames included "The Wizard of the Dribble" and "The Magician".

Matthews kept fit enough to play top-level football until he was 50 years old.

Matthews is the oldest player to play in England's top football division and the oldest player to represent the country. He was an inaugural inductee to the English Football Hall of Fame in 2002 in honour for his contribution to the English game.

MAY

1, Daisy *May*

"Daisy May" was a little schoolgirl ventriloquist's dummy used by Albert Saveen.

Saveen was the first ventriloquist with his own radio series, a post-war BBC Light Programme show called Midday with Daisy May.

The act would usually finish with this song:

"Daisy May,
People say you'll marry me one day,
And by the way you sigh,
And look me in the eye,
I somehow think that Daisy may"

2, Piggy *May*

Not a clue!

3, Maggie *May*

"Maggie May" is a song co-written with Martin Quittenton and performed by Rod Stewart from his album Every Picture Tells a Story.

Stewart recalled:

"Maggie May was more or less a true story, about the first woman I had sex with, at the 1961 Beaulieu Jazz Festival."

The woman was not "Maggie May". Stewart says that name was taken from *"... an old Liverpudlian song about a prostitute."*

It was Stewart's first hit as a solo performer, launching his solo career.

McREA

George *McRae*

1970s soul singer. George Warren McCrae, Jr. an American soul and disco singer, most famous for his 1974 hit "Rock Your Baby".

MEADOWS

Grassy *Meadows*

Play on meadows being grassy places.

METCALF

Fruity *Metcalf*

Now, this is a chap with a rather interesting career...

Edward Dudley Metcalfe MVO MC, known as 'Fruity Metcalfe', was an officer in the Indian Army and a close friend and equerry of the Prince of Wales, later King Edward VIII and Duke of Windsor.

He was commissioned on to the Unattached list for Auxiliary Forces (University Candidate) on 27 May 1907. He transferred to the Unattached List, Indian Army on 15 August 1908, but to have seniority from 17 August 1907.

He spent a year attached to the 1st battalion Connaught Rangers in India from 8 November 1908 until, on 8 November 1909, being accepted into the Indian Army and joining 3rd Skinner's Horse. He was promoted lieutenant on 17 November 1909.

On 12 August 1914, he was appointed Adjutant of the Governor's Body Guard, Bombay.

He did not hold this position for long as his regiment was mobilised to France late in 1914. He was promoted temporary captain 1 September 1915, before being sent back to India in June 1916, where he volunteered to serve with the 7th Meerut Cavalry headquarters which went to Mesopotamia.

He was Mentioned in Despatches on 15 August 1917. Ten days later he was awarded the Military Cross for distinguished service in Mesopotamia.

Metcalfe met the future Edward VIII when, as Prince of Wales, he was touring India in 1922.

Edward was impressed with Metcalfe's knowledge of horses and made him a member of his personal staff. After the king abdicated and became Duke of Windsor, Metcalfe was best man at his wedding in France to Mrs Simpson. He was his equerry from 1939 in Paris and Antibes until the German invasion of France in 1940 prompted the Windsor's' evacuation and the Duke's appointment to govern the Bahamas.

On 10 August 1940, Metcalfe was commissioned as a pilot officer into the Administrative and Special Duties Branch of the Royal Air Force. He was promoted to flying officer on 10 August 1941.

He was posted to Cairo in November 1941, returning to Britain at the end of September 1942 but resigned his commission on 17 November 1942.

MILLER/MILLAR

1, Dusty *Miller*

Play on a miller being covered in dust

2, Windy *Miller*

Play on words – windmill

MILLS

1, Bomber *Mills*

'Mills bomb' is the popular name for a series of British hand grenades.

They were the first modern fragmentation grenades used by the British Army and saw widespread use in World War I.

William Mills, a hand grenade designer from Sunderland, patented, developed and manufactured the 'Mills bomb' at the Mills Munition Factory in Birmingham, England, in 1915.

The Mills bomb was adopted by the British Army as its standard hand grenade in 1915 and designated the No. 5.

The final variation of the Mills bomb, the No. 36M was specially designed and waterproofed with shellac for use in the hot climate of Mesopotamia in 1917 but remained in production for many years.

2, Timber *Mills*

3, Saw *Mills*

4, Woody *Mills*

All variants of a similar play on words.

MUNRO, MUNROE

1, Darby *Munro*

Hugh Munro was a racehorse trainer in Victoria, closely associated with the St Albans Stud of Geelong.

He was the father of noted Sydney jockeys Jimmie Munro and Darby Munro. Circa 1903 to 1934.

2, Marilyn *Monroe*

Marilyn Monroe, born Norma Jeane Mortenson, June 1st, 1926, an American actress, model and singer. Famous for playing comic 'blonde bombshell' characters, she became one of the most popular sex symbols of the 1950s and was emblematic of the era's attitudes towards sexuality.

By 1953, Monroe was one of the most marketable Hollywood stars; she had leading roles in the noir film Niagara, which focused on her sex appeal and the comedies Gentlemen Prefer Blondes and How to Marry a Millionaire, which established her star image as a 'dumb blonde'.

Her last completed film was the drama The Misfits (1961).

She died at age 36, (on August 5, 1962), from an overdose of barbiturates at her home in Los Angeles. Although Monroe's death was ruled a probable suicide, several conspiracy theories have been proposed in the decades following her death.

MOORE

1, Pony *Moore*

Named after George Washington "Pony" Moore, a New York-born British music hall impresario, who ran the Magpie Music Hall in Battersea and later formed the Moore and Burgess Minstrels.

He was a well-known sporting character who allegedly always bet in "ponies" (*betting slang for a sum of £25*).

He died in London, England on October 1, 1909.

2, Charley *Moore*

A navy term meaning '*honest and respectable*' e.g. "*everything's Charlie Moore*".

This originates from a pub advertisement in Malta, in Victorian times, which read "Charley Moore - The Fair Thing."

MORGAN

Think Morgan Rum, think of the bottle's label...

Rattler *Morgan*

Rattle is the naval slang for prison and Henry Morgan is reputed to have always carried a large bunch of keys.

Sir Henry Morgan. (Welsh: Harri Morgan, c. 1635 – 25 August 1688), was a Welsh privateer, landowner and, later, Lieutenant Governor of Jamaica.

From his base in Port Royal, Jamaica, Morgan raided settlements and shipping on the Spanish Main. With the prize money from the raids, he purchased three large sugar plantations on the island.

Morgan became a close friend of Sir Thomas Modyford, the Governor of Jamaica. When diplomatic relations between the Kingdom of England and Spain worsened in 1667, Modyford gave Morgan a letter of marque, a licence to attack and seize Spanish vessels.

Morgan was appointed a Knight Bachelor in November 1674 and returned to Jamaica shortly after to serve as the territory's Lieutenant Governor. He served on the Assembly of Jamaica until

1683 and on three occasions acted as Governor of Jamaica in the absence of the post-holder.

He died in Jamaica on 25 August 1688. His life was romanticised after his death and he became the inspiration for pirate-themed works of fiction across a range of genres.

The single verse from C.K. Sharpe's manuscript (Charles Kirkpatrick Sharpe of Hoddam, Dumfriesshire) has an interesting note regarding Rattler...

I took her into a Brandy Shop
I gave her a Glass or two to settle her
I laid her down flat on the Broad of her Back
And lathered her up with my Morgan Rattler.

MURPHY

Spud *Murphy*

Play on Murphy being a common Irish surname in association with the Irish Potato Famine.

MURRAY

Ruby *Murry*

Ruby Florence Murray was one of the most popular singers in the United Kingdom and Ireland in the 1950s. In 1955 she secured seven Top 10 UK hit singles.

Her first single, Heartbeat, reached No. 3 in the Singles Chart (December 1954). "Softly, Softly", reached number one in early 1955. That same year Murray set a pop chart record by having five hits in the Top Twenty in one week, a feat unmatched for many years.

In 52 weeks, starting in 1955, Murray was constantly in the UK charts, at a time when only the Top 20 were listed.

I often wonder if she enjoyed a Beef Madras after the show? It would certainly answer another question!

N

NOVEMBER

NELSON

Sandy *Nelson*

One of the best-known Rock drummers of the 1950's & 60's.

Aa well as several solo top 40 hits, Sandy played with Phil Spector, Duane Eddy, Gene Vincent, The Coasters and Kathy Young and the Innocents.

Nelson continued to record even after losing a foot in a motorcycle accident in 1963.

He recorded several albums in the early 70's and in September 2008 made a recording as Sandy Nelson & the Sin City Termites (Eddie Angle, Remi Gits & Billy Favata) on the independent Spinout label.

NEW

Knocky *New*

This is a strange one. While there is no direct reference to the word 'Knocky' it is used to describe percussion, as in "*those drums sounded knocky*".

Therefore, it could be concluded that Knocky is to do with hitting, thumping or banging.

Regarding Jack, the 'banging' connection could be considered in a sexual connotation, so 'Knocky New' could be a reference to a new sexual partner, losing one's virginity... a new position or something much more perverted... Your choice!

NEWMAN

Alfie *Newman*

Commander Alfred William Newman was born at Prebendal House in Empingham, Rutland, on the 11th of April 1888. He was the second son of Miles William Newman and Jessie (née Reay). Alfred joined the Royal Navy on the 5th August 1903, aged 15.

On the 10th of October 1917, a fire alarm sounded in the after magazine of HMS Tetrarch. Alfie proceeded to the magazine and saw smoke coming from a box of cordite. He passed the cartridges to the upper deck, where they were thrown overboard. It is considered his prompt action saved the magazine from exploding and hence the loss of many lives.

Alfred was presented with the Albert Medal by King George V on the 8th of March 1918. The award published in the London Gazette.

Alfred retired from the Royal Navy in August 1922 but promoted to lieutenant commander (retired) in June 1927.

He was recalled in 1939 because of his knowledge of boom defence and served in West Africa, Aden and Malta during the second world war.

When the war ended Alfred oversaw the clearing several wrecks from Malta's Grand Harbour, including the oil tanker SS Ohio. Commander Alfie Newman retired in 1948 to East Grinstead.

He died 1 September 1984.

NOTE:

In 1971 all living holders of the Albert Medal were invited to exchange the award for the George Cross. On being exchanged, the original medal was presented to the National Maritime Museum.

The Museum also holds Alfie's George Cross and other medals on loan.

NICHOLSON

Jack *Nicholson*

Born as John Joseph Nicholson in 1937, Jack has won the Academy Award for Best Actor twice, one for One Flew Over the Cuckoo's Nest in 1975 and the other for As Good as It Gets in 1997.

He won a third Academy Award, for Best Supporting Actor, for Terms of Endearment in 1983. Nicholson is one of three male actors to win three Academy Awards.

He is one of only two actors to be nominated for an Academy Award in every decade from the 1960s to the 2000s. (The other is Michael Caine).

Jack won six Golden Globe Awards and received the Kennedy Centre Honour in 2001.

In 1994, he became one of the youngest actors to be awarded the American Film Institute's Life Achievement Award.

NOBLE

Real 'old Pusser' is this nickname.

Charlie *Noble*

Originally, Charley Noble was the matelots name for the galley chimney, which drew the heat from the galley stove and carried it safely above decks.

It was a necessary piece of equipment on ships made of wood, hemp rope and bitumen.

A British merchant seaman captain, Charles Noble, is said to be responsible for the origin of this nickname.

Around 1850, Captain Noble found the stack of his ship's galley was made of copper and ordered it be kept bright.

The ship's company began referring to it as a Charley Noble.

It is recorded, when the chimney became full of soot, the kitchen staff would fire a pistol up the stack to clear it.

This was called

"Firing Charley Noble"

NORMAN

Spiny *Norman*

A modern accepted nickname, after the Monty Python (*invisible*) character from the 'Piranha Brothers', (Doug and Dinsdale); a Monty Python sketch first seen in the first episode of the second series of Monty Python's Flying Circus, on September 15, 1970.

The 'Piranha Brothers', sociopathic criminals, employed a combination of *'violence and sarcasm'* to intimidate the London underworld and bring the city to its knees.

Dinsdale is afraid of 'Spiny Norman', a gigantic 'imaginary?' hedgehog whose reported size varied on Dinsdale's mood.

O

Oscar

OAKLEY

Annie *Oakley*

Annie Oakley was born Phoebe Ann Mosey in 1860.

Her 'amazing talent' as a sharpshooter came to light when she was 15 years old and won a shooting match against travelling-show marksman Frank E. Butler, whom she later married.

The couple joined Buffalo Bill's Wild West show a few years later.

Oakley also was variously known as "Miss Annie Oakley", "Little Sure Shot", "Little Miss Sure Shot", "Watanya Cicilla", "Phoebe Anne Oakley", "Mrs. Annie Oakley", "Mrs. Annie Butler", and "Mrs. Frank Butler".

Her death certificate gives her name as "Annie Oakley Butler".

O'NEILL

Peggy *O'Neill*

Peggy O'Neill was a curvaceous brunet starlet who played showgirl/model characters in three films, Song of the Open Road (1944), It's a Pleasure (1945) and The Hoodlum Saint (1946).

On the day she was to sign a Paramount contract, she was found dead from an overdose of sleeping pills, instigated after a violent quarrel with a screenwriter boyfriend who walked out on her.

OWENS

Jesse *Owens*

James Cleveland 'Jesse' Owens specialised in sprinting and the long jump. He was recognised during his lifetime as,

> *"Perhaps the greatest and most famous athlete in track and field history"*.

His achievement of setting three world records, and tying in another, in less than one hour at the 1935 in Ann Arbor, Michigan, has been called "the greatest 45 minutes ever in sport".

It has never been equalled.

During the Berlin Olympics, in 1936, Owens won four gold medals: 100 meters, 200 meters, long jump, and 4 × 100-meter relay.

> *He was the most successful athlete at the Games and, as a black man, was credited with,*

> *"Single-handedly crushing Hitler's myth of Aryan supremacy"*.

PAUL WHITE

P

Papa

PALMER

Pedlar *Palmer*

Palmer was born in Canning Town, London on the 19th of November in 1876. His father was the bare-knuckle boxing champion of Essex. It was also claimed Palmer's mother could beat any woman in London's East End.

As a boxer, Palmer soon gained the nickname "Box o' Tricks", reflecting his showmanship.

He became World Bantamweight Champion in 1895 beating Billy Plimmer of Birmingham. He kept his bantamweight title through five defences.

Later in life, Palmer served time in prison for manslaughter after a brawl on a train near Epsom.

In the 1940s he lived in Brighton and is buried on the western edge of the town.

His gravestone no longer stands.

PARKER

1, Nosey *Parker*

This nickname originates from a chap named Mathew Parker, who was the Archbishop of Canterbury during Queen Elizabeth the first's reign.

Parker was noted for sending detailed inquiries and instructions relating to the conduct of his diocese and, like many reformers, he was regarded as a busybody. *'One who sticks his nose into other people's business'.*

2, Nosey *Parker*

Another explanation rises from the activities of park-keepers or 'parkers' who were employed to patrol Hyde Park in the 19th century, partly to ensure lovers did not get too amorous in the bushes.

3, Nosey *Parker*

Of course, it could be from the popular postcard captioned 'The adventures of Nosey Parker'.

This referred to a (*fictional?*) peeping Tom who prowled Hyde Park.

The earliest citation in the *Oxford English Dictionary* is taken from the May 1890 issue of Belgravia Magazine.

Eric Partridge's Dictionary of Slang and Unconventional English says the phrase may be a reference to peeping Toms or nose-twitching rabbits at the Great Exhibition in Hyde Park in 1851.

4, Fezz (or Fez) *Parker*

(Nothing to do with funny red hats, like the one worn by Tommy Cooper)

Fezz is a corrupted spelling of Fess, an actor who starred in 'westerns' films during the 1950/60's, best known for his portrayals of Davy Crockett in the Walt Disney TV series and as Daniel Boone on television from 1964 to 1970.

Parker, (Fess Elisha Parker Jr.), was born in Fort Worth, Texas, and raised on a farm in Tom Green County near San Angelo.

He enlisted in the U.S. Navy in the latter part of World War II, hoping to become a pilot, but was too tall at 6 feet 6".

Fess transferred to the Marine Corps, as a radio operator serving in the South Pacific shortly before the atom bomb ended the war.

Around 1946, after discharge, he was stabbed in the neck by a driver during an argument after a minor car crash.

(Road rage?)

PARTON

Dolly *Parton*

Born Dolly Rebecca Parton Dean, in January 1946. Dolly Parton made her album debut in 1967, with her album Hello, I'm Dolly.

With steady success, both as a solo artist and with a series of duet albums with Porter Wagoner, her sales and chart peak came during the 1970s and continued into the 1980s.

In the new millennium, Parton achieved commercial success again releasing on independent labels since 2000, including her own label, Dolly Records.

She is the most honoured female country performer of all time.

As an actress, she has starred in films such as '9 to 5' and 'The Best Little Whorehouse in Texas' (1982).

PATTERSON, PATTINSON

Banjo *Patterson*

Andrew Barton 'Banjo' Paterson, CBE, was an Australian bush poet, journalist and author.

He was born at the property "Narrambla", near Orange, New South Wales, the eldest son of Andrew Bogle Paterson, a Scottish immigrant from Lanarkshire and Australian-born Rose Isabella Barton. (Related to the future first Prime Minister of Australia Edmund Barton.)

While practising as a solicitor, Paterson began writing having poetry published in The Bulletin, a literary journal with a nationalist focus. This journal provided a platform for Paterson's work, which appeared under his pseudonym of "The Banjo", the name of his favourite horse.

Paterson became a war correspondent for The Sydney Morning Herald and The Age during the Second Boer War.

His graphic accounts of the relief of Kimberley, surrender of Bloemfontein and the capture of Pretoria attracted the attention of the press in Britain. He also was a correspondent during the Boxer Rebellion.

Paterson was commissioned in the 2nd Remount Unit, Australian Imperial Force in October 1915. Serving initially in France, where he was wounded and reported MIA.

In April 1919 he was discharged from the army having risen to the rank of Major.

Paterson died of a heart attack in Sydney on 5 February 1941 aged 76.

It is Paterson who is credited to lending his nickname 'Banjo' to the egg-filled sub-roll sandwiches much loved by Royal Naval personnel and not the suggested action of wiping 'mess-medals' from the front of sailor's jersey as is often anecdotally suggested.

The following poem and further details can be found in

'The Pussers Cook Book'.

(*Which is available from Amazon*)

This is Banjo Patterson's poem.

"*I love my egg filled sandwiches*

As I sit here in the sun,

Sometimes from a loaf or

Even in a bun

I love when the egg runs down my chin

And my mates think it's a joke

I look in a nearby mirror

And I'm covered in its yolk

What could I call my sandwich

A word that will be in history

I know what I'll do mate,

I'll name it after me

Mmmmmmm, my egg filled sandwich

See the juices start to flow

I love my egg filled sandwich

My lovely Egg Banjo........."

PAYNE, PAINE

1, Whacker *Payne*

Eleazer Arthur Paine was an American soldier, author and lawyer from Ohio.

He provoked controversy as a general in the Union Army during the American Civil War and was charged with brutality toward civilians and violating their civil rights while commanding troops in western Kentucky.

2, Glassy *Payne*

3, Window *Payne*

Both a simple play on words.

PERKINS

Polly P*erkins*

From *"Pretty Polly Perkins of Paddington Green",* an English song, composed by songwriter Harry Clifton and first published in 1864.

It is catalogued as Roud Folk Song Index No. 430.

I am a broken-hearted milkman, in grief, I'm arrayed
Through keeping of the company of a young servant maid
Who lived on board and wages, the house to keep clean
In a gentleman's family near Paddington Green

She was as beautiful as a butterfly and proud as a Queen
Was pretty little Polly Perkins of Paddington Green

She'd an ankle like an antelope and a step like a deer
A voice like a blackbird, so mellow and clear
Her hair hung in ringlets so beautiful and long
I thought that she loved me, but I found I was wrong

[Alternative and possibly original/earlier lyrics to second verse]

Her eyes were as black as the pips of a pear
No rose in the garden with her cheeks could compare
Her hair hung in ringlets so beautiful and long
I thought that she loved me, but I found I was wrong

Refrain

When I'd rattle in the morning and cry "Milk below"
At the sound of my milk cans her face she did show
With a smile upon her countenance and a laugh in her eye
If I'd thought that she loved me I'd have laid down to die

Refrain

When I asked her to marry me, she said "Oh what stuff"
And told me to stop it for she'd had quite enough
Of my nonsense... At the same time, I'd been very kind
But to marry a milkman she didn't feel inclined

Refrain

"The man that has me must have silver and gold
A chariot to ride in and be handsome and bold
His hair must be curly as any watch-spring,
And his whiskers as big as a brush for clothing"

Refrain

The words that she uttered went straight through my heart
I sobbed, and I sighed, and I straight did depart
With a tear on my eyelid as big as a bean
I bid farewell to Polly and to Paddington Green

Refrain

In six months she married, this hard-hearted girl
But it was not a viscount, and it was not an earl
It was not a baronite, but a shade or two worse
It was a bow-legged conductor of a tuppenny bus

Refrain

PHILLPOTTS

An original Royal Naval derivation

Putty *Phillpotts/Philpots*

Putty is simply the old name for a ship's painter, one who often used and mixed putty and/or was in charge of the ships paint store.

The term *'On the Putty'* was one also used for a ship which had run aground.

I have not been able to ascertain who the original 'Putty' was, but my guess is it was a general nickname given to the ship's painter *until* a Captain named Phillpotts ran his ship aground, after which Jack delighted calling all named Phillpotts 'Putty'.

POOLE

Cess *Pool/Sess Pool*

A play on words.

POTTER

1, Gillie *Potter*

1940s/50s radio comic who spoke with a mock superior air. His catchphrase was "Good evening, England. This is Gillie Potter speaking to you, in English".

Potter was born in Bedford to Reverend Brignal Peel, a Wesleyan minister, and Elizabeth Stimson.

He first performed in E. M. Royle's The White Man at the Lyric Theatre in London.

During the Great War (WW1), Potter served as a 2nd lieutenant in the 6th Division 2nd Brigade 21st Battery, Royal Field Artillery in France.

Potter cultivated an individual style and persona, wearing a straw boater, wide grey flannel trousers (It has been said he invented the 'Oxford bags' style of trouser in 1920), an 'Old Borstolian' blazer, carried a notebook and a rolled umbrella.

He became one of the most popular radio entertainers in Britain.

2, Pansy *Potter*

'Pansy Potter, The Strongman's Daughter' a comic strip created by Hugh McNeill for the children's comic, The Beano.

Pansy Potter is a girl with super strength.

In 2012 Pansy returned to The Beano in the 'Funsize Funnies' section, drawn by Nigel Parkinson. She returned for a second run later, where she was drawn and written by Kev F. Sutherland.

3, Harry *Potter (Modern)*

The latest incarnation of the 'Potter' nickname is JK Rowling's Novel(s) character of a young wizard called Harry Potter.

The novels chronicle the life of a young wizard, Harry Potter and his friends Hermione Granger and Ron Weasley, all of whom are students at Hogwarts School of Witchcraft and Wizardry.

As of February 2018, the books have sold more than 500 million copies worldwide, making them the best-selling book series in history.

They have been translated into eighty languages.

POWELL

1, Cozy *Powell*

Colin Trevor "Cozy" Powell, an English rock drummer, made his name playing in major rock bands, The Jeff Beck Group, Rainbow, Gary Moore, Robert Plant, Brian May, Whitesnake, Emerson - Lake & Powell, and Black Sabbath.

Powell appeared on over 66 albums and contributed to many other recordings. He is cited as a major influence in the music business.

2, Sandy *Powell*

"Sandy" Powell MBE, a pre- and post-war comedian who coined the catchphrase "Can you hear me Mother?" in the 1930s.

Fifty years later, deciding he needed a rest from the business, he again said it in a Coventry theatre for the last time.

PRICE

Prickly *Price*

No definitive documented relationship found.

R

Romeo

RAMSEY

Alf *Ramsey*

Sir Alfred Ernest Ramsey, an English football player and manager who, as manager of the England national football team from 1963 to 1974, guided England to victory in the 1966 FIFA World Cup.

Ramsey also managed England to third place in the 1968 European Championship and the quarter-finals of the 1970 World Cup and the 1972 European Championship respectively.

As a player, Ramsey was a defender and a member of England's 1950 World Cup squad.

He remains widely regarded as one of British football's all-time great managers.

RAY

1, Manta *Ray*/Sting *Ray*

A play on words.

2, Sting Ray

Gerry and Sylvia Anderson created a children's 'Supermarionation' television series called Stingray.

Its 39 episodes aired between 1964 and 1965. There are also two Stingray 'specials' and two compilation films (1980 & 1981).

Stingray was the first Supermarionation production in which the marionette characters had interchangeable heads featuring a variety of expressions.

It was also the first British television series to be filmed entirely in colour.

Stingray, a highly sophisticated combat submarine built for speed and manoeuvrability is the flag vessel of the World Aquanaut Security Patrol (WASP), a security organisation based at Marineville in the year 2065.

REED, REID

1, Blood *Reed/Reid*

A simple play on words. Reid (Reed) translating as Red in Scottish & Gaelic.

2, Pricky *Reed*

Unknown as with Pricky Price.

REYNOLDS

1, Burt *Reynolds*

Burton Leon Reynolds Jr, actor, director, producer and former American football player. He first rose to prominence starring in television series Gunsmoke, from 1962 to '65 and Dan August 1970 to '71.

His breakout role was playing a character called Lewis Medlock in Deliverance 1972.

Burts other films include The Longest Yard, Smokey and the Bandit, Semi-Tough, Hooper, Smokey and the Bandit II, The Cannonball Run and The Best Little Whorehouse in Texas (with Dolly Parton).

2, Debbie *Reynolds*

Female singer, cinema and TV star; Mary Frances "Debbie" Reynolds whose first leading role, as Kathy Selden in Singin' in the Rain, established her as a star.

Her other films include The Singing Nun, Divorce American Style, What's the Matter with Helen? Charlotte's Web, Mother and In & Out.

Reynolds reached a new generation as Aggie Cromwell in Disney's Halloweentown. In 1988, she released her autobiography Debbie: My Life. In 2013, she released a second autobiography, Unsinkable: A Memoir.

On December 28, 2016, Reynolds was hospitalized at Cedars-Sinai Medical Centre following a medical emergency, which her son Todd Fisher later described as a "severe stroke".

She died from the stroke that afternoon, one day after the death of her daughter Carrie Fisher.

RHODES

Dusty *Rhodes*

A play on words, (*dusty roads*), but attributed to Jonathan Neil 'Jonty' Rhodes a South African international cricketer, known as 'Dusty' Rhodes in Britain.

Dusty is regarded as one of the greatest fielders of all time. He played for the South African cricket team between 1992 and 2003.

RIDER

Easy *Rider*

Easy Rider is a 1969 American independent road drama film written by Peter Fonda, Dennis Hopper and Terry Southern. It was produced by Fonda and directed by Hopper.

Two bikers, (motorcyclists), travel through America's Southwest and South carrying the proceeds from a drug deal.

Easy Rider explores the societal landscape, issues and tensions in the United States during the 1960s, such as the rise of the hippie movement, drug use and communal lifestyle.

Real drugs were used in scenes showing the use of marijuana and other substances.

The film was added to the Library of Congress National Film Registry in 1998.

RIDD

Jan *Ridd*

A character from the novel "Lorna Doone" by R D Blackmore. Set in 17th-century Badgworthy Water in Devon.

John, *pronounced "Jan" in West Country dialect*, Ridd is the son of a respectable farmer who was murdered by one of the notorious Doone clan, (a once noble family, who are now outlaws), in the isolated Doone Valley.

Jan Ridd helps Lorna escape to his family's farm, Plover's Barrows. King Charles II dies and the Duke of Monmouth challenges Charles's brother James for the throne.

Jan Ridd is captured during the revolution. Innocent of all charges, he is taken to London by an old friend to clear his name.

There, he is reunited with Lorna whose love for him has not diminished. When he thwarts an attack on Lorna's great-uncle and legal guardian Earl Brandir, Jan is granted a pardon, a title, and a coat of arms by the king and returns a free man to Exmoor.

Yippie doo.

RIDDLE

Jimmy *Riddle*

Slang. From the Cockney rhyming slang, 'Jimmy Riddle – piddle'.

This term is mentioned in Partridge's A Dictionary of Slang and Unconventional English, 1937.

It is listed as *'late 19th century'*.

Several 'Jimmy' phrases were coined in the 19th century; for example,

A, Jimmy Grant (immigrant/emigrant)

B, Jimmy Ducks - a sailor in charge of livestock onboard ship. This is a similar coinage to that of a character working in the prison kitchens in the BBC comedy Porridge - *'Luke Warm'.*

C, Jimmy Woods - someone who drinks alone.

D, Jimmy O'Goblin - a sovereign.

These use the name 'Jimmy' as a generic man's name, much as Londoners and others now use the name 'John'.
It is most probably how 'Jimmy Riddle' was derived too.

RODGERS

Buck *Rodgers*

Buck Rogers is a fictional space opera character created by Philip Francis Nowlan in the novella 'Armageddon 2419 A.D.'

The strip made its first newspaper appearance on January 7, 1929.

Later adaptations included a film serial, a television series and other formats.

Buck Rogers is credited with bringing the concept of space exploration into popular media, following in the footsteps of literary pioneers such as Jules Verne, H. G. Wells and Edgar Rice Burroughs.

ROSS

Albert *Ross*

A play on the word, 'Albatross'.

It is considered unlucky to kill an albatross; in Coleridge's poem, the narrator killed the bird and his fellow sailors eventually force him to wear the dead bird around his neck.

The albatross as a superstitious relic is referenced in Samuel Taylor Coleridge's well-known epic poem, *The Rime of the Ancient Mariner*.

ROYLE

Joe *Royle*

Joseph Royle played centre-forward for Everton football club during the 1970's. He is, at the time the of writing, a football manager.

In club career, he played for Everton, (debuting at the age of 16), Manchester City, Bristol City, Norwich City and the England national team.

As a manager for Oldham Athletic, Everton, Manchester City and Ipswich Town.

He is a patron of Zöe's Place Baby Hospice, a charity for sick babies and young children.

RUSHTON

Willy *Rushton*

William George Rushton, an English cartoonist, satirist, comedian, actor and performer who co-founded the satirical magazine, Private Eye.

RYAN

Buck *Ryan*

Monk and Freeman were doing an adaptation of Edgar Wallace's Terror Keep for the Daily Mirror.

When it was dropped due to a rights problem, Monk and Freeman decided to fashion their own strip, and Buck Ryan was born.

It ran in the Daily Mirror from 22 March 1937 to July 1962.

Buck Ryan started again in the Daily Mirror 3 August 2015.

PAUL WHITE

S

Sierra

SAUNDERS

Sandy *Saunders*

One of the longest surviving members of a group of World War Two pilots who underwent pioneering plastic surgery.

> *Along with other wounded veterans who were given experimental skin grafts, they were dubbed the*
>
> *'Guinea Pig Club'.*

Sandy was a 22-year-old pilot at the time of his crash. He underwent 28 operations to treat the 40% burns to his face, hands and legs.

Pioneering surgeon Sir Archibald McIndoe carried out the experimental plastic surgery techniques, some of which are still in use today.

(Sir Archibald Hector McIndoe CBE FRCS, a pioneering New Zealand plastic surgeon who worked for the Royal Air Force during the Second World War. He greatly improved the treatment and rehabilitation of badly burned aircrew.)

Dr (Sandy) Saunders was inspired to become a GP by Sir Archibald and worked as a doctor in Nottingham for 40 years.

SHACKLETON

Bomber *Shackleton*

The Avro Shackleton was developed during the late 1940s as part of Britain's military response to the rapid expansion of the Soviet Navy and its submarine force.

In April 1951, it entered operational service with the RAF.

The Shackleton main role was anti-submarine warfare (ASW) and as a maritime patrol aircraft (MPA). it was also frequently deployed in aerial search and rescue (SAR) and occasionally as a crude troop-transport aircraft.

In the 1970s, the Shackleton was replaced by the jet-powered Hawker Siddeley Nimrod. Although a small number of Shackleton's received extensive modifications to perform the airborne early warning (AEW) and continued in this support capacity until 1991 when replaced by the newer Boeing E-3 Sentry AEW aircraft.

SHARPE

Razor *Sharpe*

Play on words. Razors need to be sharp. (*But not all matelots are*).

SHAW

Artie *Shaw*

Regarded as 'one of jazz's finest clarinettists', Shaw led one of the popular big bands of the 1930/40s.

He served in the US Navy from 1942 to 1944.

Following his discharge, he returned to lead a band through to 1945, when he withdrew from the limelight.

Shaw remained associated with jazz before retiring completely.

Shaw died in December 2004.

SHEPHERD

Jack *Shepherd*

Jack Sheppard was a notorious English thief and gaol (*jail*) breaker of early 18th-century London.

Born into a poor family, he was apprenticed as a carpenter but took to theft and burglary.

He was arrested and imprisoned five times in 1724, escaping four times, making him a notorious public figure, one who was wildly popular with the poorer class.

Ultimately, he was caught, convicted and hanged at Tyburn, ending his brief criminal career in less than two years.

There are several 'Jack Shepherd's which individuals lay claim they are named after and who am I to argue?

However, my research suggests it is this notorious criminal 'Jack Shepherd' whose name is the original one used as a Naval nickname.

SHERMAN

Tank/Tanky *Sherman*

A name given after the world war two tank, the M4 Sherman, which in turn is named after the American Civil War general William T. Sherman. It is one of the few truly iconic fighting vehicles of the Allies during World War Two and one of the most famous tanks in history.

SHORT

Jumper *Short*

1, Possibly the longest distance a Matelot could jump?

2, The word 'Jumper' is derived from the French noun 'jump', a modified form of the French 'jupe', used to mean a short coat, (*Circa 19th century*).

It does not take too much imagination to consider the matelots 'Blue Jumper' belonging to No1's & No2's uniforms, as these are such short coats.

Are these the original 'Short Jumpers' given to this nickname? I consider it most likely regarding the results of my research into the subject as, from early Saxon times, most English wool was exported. In the early 16th century, it was sent to Calais, *(then an English possession)*, where it was woven into cloth.

NOTE:

Denim, a cotton fabric with a similar weave is believed to be derived from "Serge de Nîmes" after Nîmes in France.

Hence, Denim – 'de Nime'.

SLAUGHTER

Tod *Slaughter*

Tod Slaughter, an English actor, best known for playing over-the-top maniacs in macabre film melodramas.

After a brief interruption to serve during World War I in the Royal Flying Corps, Slaughter resumed his career and returned to the stage.

SLONE

Tod *Slone*

James Forman "Tod" Sloan was an American jockey. He became famous in Britain after 1897 for his unusual riding style and winning several Classics.

He was elected to the National Museum of Racing and Hall of Fame in 1955.

SMITH/SMYTH

1, Smouch Smith

When tea first arrived in Britain from China in the 1660s it was extremely expensive. Customs duties were added the following century, which encouraged smuggling and counterfeiting.

Often these 'fake' teas, made of dried hawthorn, sloe or ash leaves were often coloured with noxious substances like Verdigris and copperas. These were sold under the slang name of 'Smouch'.

Although the source is unclear, the term came to mean *'to pilfer or acquire by dishonest means'* as in the novel Huckleberry Finn by Mark Twain:

"Now, there's SENSE in that," I says. "Letting on don't cost nothing; letting on ain't no trouble; and if it's any object, I don't mind letting on we was at it a hundred and fifty year. It wouldn't strain me none, after I got my hand in. So, I'll mosey along now, and smouch a couple of case-knives."

"Smouch three," he says; "we want one to make a saw out of."

"Tom, if it ain't unregular and irreligious to sejest it," I says, "there's an old rusty saw-blade around yonder sticking under the weather-boarding behind the smoke-house."

He looked kind of weary and discouraged-like, and says:

"It ain't no use to try to learn you nothing, Huck. Run along and smouch the knives -- three of them." So, I done it.

2, Smudge/Smudger *Smith*

Much as the above, also linked to the word 'Smutch'. Basically, derivations of making things, (or referring to things), which can be considered 'dirty'.

The connection to the surname Smith or Smyth is unclear, but it could have a blacksmithing connection as many associated words, such as smutt, smutty, smutch, smittled, smooched, etc. all refer to similar reference.

SNOW

Frosty *Snow*

Hum

Hmph, it does not take a genius to work this one out.

SPEAR

Chukka Spear

Quite a clever play on words.

STEEL

1, Rusty *Steel*

2, Shiny *Steel*

Simply wordplay.

STEPHENS

Stainless *Stephens*

Arthur Clifford Baynes, an English teacher and comedian from Sheffield, Yorkshire, performed under the stage name 'Stainless' Stephen.

He appeared in a tuxedo, a bowler hat with a steel band around it, a rotating bow tie and a stainless-steel vest.

During WWI he served in the Sheffield City Battalion.

This is Stainless aimless brainless Stephen, semi-colon, broadcasting semi-conscious at the microphone semi-frantic.

Closing a broadcast on 22 March 1941, he said:

"And so, countrymen, semi-colon, all shoulders to the wheel, semi-quaver, we'll carry on till we get the Axis semi-circle, and Hitler asks us for a full stop!"

As a postscript to his career Stainless Stephen appeared as a guest on Frost on Saturday on ITV on 15 November 1969.

This edition was dedicated to the history of British Broadcasting to mark the first evening of colour transmissions on ITV.

In the show, the comedian gave the television audience a sample of his somewhat unusual comedy routine.

This programme survives intact in the ITV archives.

Stainless died in Chiddingstone, Kent in 1971.

STONE

1, Rocky *Stone*

Simple, think about it... but not for too long.

2, Jed *Stone*

John Edward "Jed" Stone is a fictional character from the British ITV soap opera, Coronation Street.

Played by Kenneth Cope, he was a lodger of Minnie Caldwell's in the 1960s, her nickname for him was "Sunny Jim".

SULLIVAN

Spike *Sullivan*

A contraction.

SUMMERVILLE

1, Slim *Summerville*

George Joseph Somerville, known professionally as Slim Summerville, was American actor best known as a comedy performer.

2, Jimmy *Summerville* (Modern)

Scottish pop singer and songwriter.

He sang in the 1980s with the pop groups Bronski Beat and The Communards, he also has a solo career.

T & U

Tango & Uniform

TANNER

Elsie *Tanner*

Elsie Tanner, (also *Gregory, Grimshaw, and Howard*) is a fictional character from the British ITV soap opera, Coronation Street, played by Pat Phoenix from the series inception in 1960 to 1973 and again from 1976 until 1984.

TARRANT

Spider *Tarrant*

As in 'Tarantella' the spider species.

TAYLOR, TAYLOR/TAILOR

1, Buck *Taylor*

Walter Clarence Taylor the III, known as Buck Taylor is known for his role as gunsmith-turned-deputy, Newly O'Brien in 174 episodes of the 'Gunsmoke' television series (1967–1975).

Taylor's painting speciality is the American West, and each year, he creates the posters for several Texas rodeos. Taylor lives with his second wife on a ranch near Fort Worth, Texas.

2, Snip *Taylor*

Scissors, cut, snip... it is not too difficult to work this one out.

THATCHER

Maggie/Maggs/Maggot *Thatcher*

After Margaret Hilda Thatcher, (née Roberts), later Baroness Thatcher, LG, OM, PC, FRS, FRIC.

She served as Prime Minister from 1979 to 1990 and Leader of the Conservative Party from 1975 to 1990.

She is the longest-serving British prime minister of the 20th century and the first woman to have been appointed.

THOMAS

Tommy/Tomo *Thomas*

Diminutives.

TICKLE

Tess *Tickles*

Reference to the male genitalia.

TODD

Sweeny *Todd*

Sweeney Todd is a fictional character who first appeared as the villain of the Victorian penny dreadful 'The String of Pearls' Cira 1846–47. The tale became a staple of Victorian melodrama and London urban legend.

In the original version of the tale, Todd is a barber who dispatches his victims by pulling a lever as they sit in his barber chair. His victims fall backwards down a revolving trapdoor into the basement of his shop causing them to break their necks or skulls. In case they remain alive, Todd 'polishes them off' by slitting their throats with his straight (*cutthroat*) razor.

After Todd robs his victims, Mrs Lovett, his partner in crime (*in some later versions, his friend and/or lover*), assists him in disposing of the bodies by baking making them into meat pies and selling them to the unsuspecting customers of her pie shop.

TRUEMAN

1, Ben *Truman*

Joseph Truman inherited the Lolsworth Field brewery, William Bucknall's Brewhouse, in 1694 and took his son into partnership in 1722.

"On the birth of the Duchess of Brunswick, granddaughter of George II, in August 1737, the Prince of Wales ordered four loads of faggots and a number of tar barrels to be burnt before Carlton House to celebrate the event and directed the brewer of his household to place four barrels of beer near the bonfire for the use of those who chose to partake of the beverage.

The beer proved to be of inferior quality and the people threw it into each other's faces and the barrels into the fire.

The prince remedied the matter on the following night by ordering a fresh quantity of beer from another brewer. This was supplied by Truman, who took care that it should be of the best, thus earning for himself considerable popularity".

Under Truman's management, the Black Eagle brewery increased substantially in prosperity and size. Truman divided his time between the brewery's Directors' House and Popes, in Hertfordshire.

Truman was knighted by George III on his accession in 1760 in recognition of his loyalty (in contributing to the voluntary loans raised to carry on the various foreign wars). His portrait, painted by Sir Thomas Gainsborough, has been part of the Tate Gallery collection since 1978.

2, Fred *Truman*

Frederick Sewards Trueman, an English cricketer who became a popular broadcaster.

Fred was a right-handed batsman and right-arm fast bowler who played for Yorkshire and England.

He is generally acknowledged as one of the greatest bowlers in cricket history. He was the first bowler to take 300 wickets in Test cricket.

He was awarded the OBE in the 1989 Queen's Birthday Honours for services to cricket.

TUCKER

Tommy *Tucker*

Originally from the nursery rhyme character. *"Little Tommy Tucker".*

It has a Roud Folk Song Index number of 19618

Common modern versions include:

Little Tom Tucker
Sings for his supper.
What shall we give him?
White bread and butter.
How shall he cut it
Without a knife?
How will he be married
Without a wife?

NOTE:

In medieval times it was customary for a hungry singer or entertainer arriving at local inn or bar to offer some songs, to tell a tale or recite poetry, hence entertaining the customers, in return for a meal. Later in the 17th century, the phrase came to mean to perform some task or do a service in order get your desire fulfilled or to earn something that you needed.

TURNER

1, Topsy *Turner*

Possibly related to the saying "to turn topsy-turvy" when upsetting something or falling over.

2, Tina *Turner* (Modern)

'Turner' was born, Anna Mae Bullock to a small family in Nutbush, Tennessee.

She began singing with local church choirs.

Her career began in 1958 as a featured singer with Ike Turner's Kings of Rhythm.

She first recorded under the name of "Little Ann".

Tina is one of the world's best-selling artists, she has been referred to as The Queen of Rock 'n' Roll, selling more than 200 million albums and singles worldwide. According to Guinness World Records, she has sold more concert tickets than any other solo performer in history.

TYLER

Bonnie *Tyler*

Bonnie Tyler, born Gaynor Hopkins, is a Welsh singer known for her distinctive husky voice.

She came to prominence with the release of her 1977 album The World Starts Tonight and its singles 'Lost in France' and 'More Than a Lover'. Her 1978 single 'It's a Heartache' reached number four on the UK Singles Chart and number three on the US Billboard Hot 100.

PAUL WHITE

V & W

Victor & Whiskey

VAUGHAN

Guy *Vaughan*

Unknown. No connection found.

WALKER

1, Hooky/Hookey/hookee *Walker*

Most probably taken from... John Walker, 'an outdoor clerk' at Longman, Clementi and Co.'s in Cheapside, London.

Walker sported a hooked nose and, it is rumoured, he spied on his fellow employees for 'the nobs of the firm'.

Those he spied on declared his reports were nonsense and, since they outnumbered Walker, their denials tended to prevail.

This version is however contested; the alternatives being a Magistrate of the same name and a gentleman of 'Jewish origin' who exhibited an orrery 'the Eidoranion' along which he would 'take a sight', which action, using an extended arm and a finger raised to the eye, was the equivalent of a dismissive gesture.

BTW:

(An orrery is a mechanical model of the solar system that shows the relative positions and motions of the planets and moons according to the heliocentric model).

2, Whisky *Walker &* **3,** Johnny *Walker*

Both after the brand of Scotch whisky now owned by Diageo which originated in the Scottish town of Kilmarnock, in East Ayrshire.

The brand was first established by grocer John Walker.

It is the most widely distributed brand of blended Scotch whisky in the world, sold in almost every country, with annual sales of the equivalent of over 223.7 million 700 ml bottles in 2016 (156.6 million litres).

WALLACE

Nelly *Wallace*

Nellie Wallace, music hall star and one of the best-loved music hall performers.

She became known as "The Essence of Eccentricity".

Nellie was Glaswegian. Her father, Francis George Tayler, was a vocalist and musician, her mother a retired actress who became a teacher and governess.

Nellie's prime character was a frustrated spinster, singing ribald songs such as 'Under the Bed,' 'Let's Have a Tiddley at the Milk Bar' and 'Mother's Pie Crust.'

Other songs in her repertoire included: 'The Sniff Song,' 'Three Cheers for the Red White & Blue,' 'The Blasted Oak,' 'Three Times a Day and 'Bang! Bang! Bang!'

> She generally wore a fur stole, which she described as her
>
> *"little bit of vermin"*

PAUL WHITE

Three Cheers for Red, White and Blue

A young man has throwed me. No wonder I'm sad

Young girls like myself, have you ever been had?

By man, the deceiver, I've been put upon

Lor' knows, I'm a trier, I ought to get on

I've nearly been married three times, it's a fact

But the love of my lover turned sour

My name being Rose single men, here's a chance

While the bloom is still bright on the flower

Chorus:

I've been jilted by the baker, Mr White

A soldier and a sailor too

They've all gone astray, and yet the people say

Three cheers for the red, white and blue

The baker was nice, but he worried me so

He was always hard up and needing the dough

The thing that had captured his heart he once said

Was the bun that I wear at the back of my head

The soldier would never take me in the light

So, we spooned in a nice shady wood

One dark night he borrowed my purse and remarked

That the change, it might do him some good

Chorus:

The sailor would nurse me while smoking his shag

I'd squeeze him and call him My Little Blue Bag

Whenever he looked at my beautiful form

He'd murmur, "Well, any old port in a storm"

He said to me, "Beauty is only skin deep

And although I must now get afloat

You may be all right when I come back again

When you've moulted and shedded your coat".

Chorus:

Nellie Wallace died in a London nursing home on 24 November 1948, aged 78, after a serious bout of bronchitis.

WALTON

After, John-boy Walton, a character from the TV series *'The Waltons',* based on Earl Hamner Jr's book, *'Spencer's Mountain'* (and a 1963 film of the same name), about a family in rural Virginia during the Great Depression and World War II.

WARD

Sharkey *Ward*

While the precise origin of nickname 'Sharkey' is unrecorded, as seafarers it does not stretch one's imagination why this 'John Ward', whose real name was Yusuf Rais, was given or adopted the name in the early 1600's.

Sharkey Ward was an English sea captain turned Barbary Corsair. He was based in Tunis, (where he died of the plague).

It is alleged, during Sharkey's younger years, he served on a ship caught in the crossfire of pirate ships in a battle against a Spanish galleon in which his captain was killed. He assumed position at the wheel and led his crew to safety.

Around 1603, he was pressed into service on a ship sailing under the authority of the King (*the Royal Navy had yet to become a formal institution*) and placed in the Channel Fleet aboard 'Lyon's Whelp'.

He, in a group of 30 deserted and stole a 25-ton barque from Portsmouth Harbour.

Sharkey's comrades elected him captain, one of the earliest precedents for pirates choosing their own leader. They sailed to the Isle of Wight, capturing 'The Violet', (*which Ward promptly renamed Little John*). Sharkey used her to capture a larger French ship and sailed to the Mediterranean where he acquired a warship of thirty-two guns. He renamed this ship 'The Gift' and began attacking merchantmen.

Sometime later, he accepted Islam, along with his entire crew, changing his name to Yusuf Reis and married an Italian woman, but continued to send money to his estranged English wife.

The ballad. 'Captain Ward and the Rainbow' is said to be based on the life of Jack 'Sharkey' Ward.

An English sailor who saw him in Tunis in 1608 allegedly described Ward as,

"Very short with little hair and that quite white, bald in front; swarthy face and beard. Speaks little and almost always swearing. Drunk from morn till night... The habits of a thorough salt. A fool and an idiot out of his trade."

THE ANDREW, JACK & JENNY

'Captain Ward and the Rainbow'

Come all you gallant seamen bold,
All you that march to drum,
Let's go and look for Captain Ward,
Far on the sea he roams;
He is the biggest robber
That ever you did hear,
There's not been such a robber found
For above this hundred year.

A ship was sailing from the east
And going to the west,
Loaded with silks and satins
And velvets of the best,
But meeting there with Captain Ward,
It proved a bad meeting;
He robbèd them of all their wealth
And bid them tell their king.

O then the king provided a ship of noble fame,
She's call'd the "Royal Rainbow,"

If you would know her name;
She was as well provided for
As any ship could be,
Full thirteen hundred men on board
To bear her company.

'Twas eight o' clock in the morning
When they began to fight,
And so, they did continue there
Till nine o' clock at night.
"Fight on, fight on," says Captain Ward,
"This sport well pleases me,
For if you fight this month or more,
Your master I will be."

O then the gallant "Rainbow"
She fired, she fired in vain,
Till six and thirty of her men
All on the deck were slain.
"Go home, go home," says Captain Ward,
"And tell your king from me,
If he reigns king on all the land,

Ward will reign king on sea!"

WARDLE

Sharkey *Wardle*

A derivative of the above.

WARNER

Plum *Warner*

Sir Pelham Francis Warner, affectionately known as Plum Warner or 'the Grand Old Man' of English cricket.

A right-hand batsman, Warner played cricket for Oxford University, Middlesex and England. He was named Wisden Cricketer of the Year in 1904 and in 1921, making him one of two to have received the honour twice (*the usual practice is that it is only won once: the other is Jack Hobbs*). The second award marked his retirement as a county player after the 1920 season, in which he captained Middlesex to the County Championship title.

In the mid-1920s he was Chairman of Selectors. He did not, however, play in another first-class fixture until 1926–27, when he captained a Marylebone Cricket Club (MCC) side to Argentina.

He played one more first-class match, in 1929 for the MCC against the Royal Navy.

WARREN

Bunny *Warren*

Where rabbits live.

WATERS

1, Stormy *Waters*

2, Muddy *Waters*

Play on words – rough seas etc.

WATSON

1, Soapy *Watson*

2, Sudz *Watson*

After the brand of soap issued to the Fleet.

Joseph Watson and Sons, founded by Joseph Watson Senior, grew out of a hide tanning business established around 1820, at Woodside, Horsforth, Leeds. (*Roughly the area between today's Outwood Lane and Broadway*).

Joseph Watson, the grandson, turned the company from a medium-sized concern into one which ruled the soap market of North-East England, with national and international markets, becoming Lever Brothers biggest rival.

By 1881 'Watsons' employed 50 men and 25 boys.

In 1906, the formation of the 'soap combine', involving more than 20 firms including Lever Brothers, took place at a meeting in the offices of Joseph Watson and Sons, Leeds.

Watson had already disposed of much of his shareholding, previously held by himself and his uncle Charles, to William Lever, in exchange for Lever Brothers shares to set up the trust.

In 1912/13 Watson sold much of his remaining shareholding to Lever Brothers, selling the remainder in July 1917, but remained as Chairman.

WEB(B)

Spider *Webb*

Self-evident, spiders make webs.

WELCH

Raquel *Welch*

Raquel Welch's real name is Jo Raquel Tejada. She was born in September 1904.

Raquel first role was in Fantastic Voyage in 1966, after which she won a contract with 20th Century Fox.

They lent her contract to a British studio, for whom she made One Million Years B.C. 1966.

She had only three lines in the film, yet images of her wearing a doe-skin bikini became best-selling posters that turned her into a celebrity sex symbol.

She carved out a place in movie history portraying strong female characters and breaking the mould of the submissive sex symbol.

WELLINGTON

Duke *Wellington*

Duke of Wellington, victor of the Battle of Waterloo in 1815.

Arthur Wellesley, 1st Duke of Wellington, KG, GCB, GCH, PC, FRS, was an Anglo-Irish soldier and statesman who was one of the leading military and political figures of 19th-century Britain.

His defeat of Napoleon at the Battle of Waterloo in 1815 puts him in the first rank of Britain's military heroes.

Wellington is famous for his adaptive defensive style of warfare, resulting in several victories against numerically superior forces while minimising his own losses.

He is regarded as one of the greatest defensive commanders of all time, and many of his tactics and battle plans are still studied in military academies around the world.

After the end of his active military career, Wellington returned to politics.

He was twice British prime minister as part of the Tory party: from 1828 to 1830, and for a little less than a month in 1834. He oversaw the passage of the Catholic Relief Act 1829 but opposed the Reform Act 1832. He continued as one of the leading figures in the House of Lords until his retirement and remained Commander-in-Chief of the British Army until his death.

Wellington Boots are named after the Duke of Wellington.

WELLS

1, Bomber *Wells*

After Bomber or more correctly "Bombardier" or "Battling" Billy Wells the British heavyweight boxing champion 1911-19.

In 1911 Bomber became the first Heavyweight to win the Lonsdale Belt, newly introduced for British champions at all weights, in 1909.

He was so well known, the big gun in the 1914-18 war was nicknamed after him.

NOTE:

My bet is you have seen 'Bomber Wells' frequently yourself while watching movies at the cinema or on your own television.

He is the man hitting the giant gong at the beginning of many Rank films.

2, Kitty *Wells*

Ellen Muriel Deason, known professionally as Kitty Wells, was a female country music singer.

She broke down a female barrier in country music with her 1952 hit recording, 'It Wasn't God Who Made Honky Tonk Angels', which made her the first female country singer to top the U.S. country charts. Turning her into the first female country star.

3, Rowdy *Wells*

Cowboy stuff...

Unknown origin, but I suspected the name was adopted from the film 'The Dogfighters' from 1966. The protagonist character is one 'Rowdy Wells'.

WEST

More cowboy stuff...

1, Banjo *West*

No provenance. Possibly to do with the popularity of cowboy films in the late 1950's and 1960's.

2, Fred *West* (Modern)

Frederick Walter Stephen West, serial killer who committed at least 12 murders between 1967 and 1987 in Gloucestershire, the majority with his second wife, Rosemary West.

All the victims were young women. Eight of the murders involved the Wests' sexual gratification, including rape, bondage, torture and mutilation; the victims' dismembered bodies were typically buried in the cellar or garden of the Wests' Cromwell Street home in Gloucester, which became known as the "House of Horrors".

Fred is known to have committed at least two murders on his own, while Rose is known to have murdered Fred's stepdaughter, Charmaine.

The pair were apprehended and charged in 1994.

Fred West asphyxiated himself while on remand at HM Prison Birmingham on 1 January 1995, at which time he and Rose were jointly charged with nine murders, he with three additional murders. In November 1995, Rose was convicted of ten murders and sentenced to ten life terms with a whole life order.

WESTON

This one deserves a long elucidation.

Aggie *Weston*

Dame Agnes Weston founded the ' Royal Sailors Rest', (*Devonport in 1876*), close to the gates of the Dockyard. It opened officially on the 8th May 1876. The various 'Rests' came because of a request for a temperance house, a "bar without drink", a sailor could go to for recreation and relaxation.

In the 1890's Agnes Weston was granted a Royal Warrant by Queen Victoria, so future the Rests were known as the 'Royal Sailors' Rests'. Queen Victoria invited Miss Weston to visit her at Windsor, in which she let her know: *"I do not forget to pray for you".*

In the same decade, Aggie created a 'Naval Disaster Fund', to care for the wives and their families, as a response to the loss of HMS SERPENT and all the ship's company.

In 1901, Agnes Weston received the honour of a degree of Doctor of Laws at Glasgow University, the first woman ever to do so.

Aggie passed away on the morning of the 23rd October 1918, shortly before the end of the First World War. Before she died, Agnes Weston was elevated to the honour of Dame Grand Cross of the Most Excellent Order of the British Empire. She was the first woman ever to be buried with full naval honours.

Over 2000 officers and men crowded into Weston Mill cemetery to pay their respects. For over half a century she had been known to countless sailors as; 'Mother Weston,' 'the Mother of the Navy,' 'The Navy's Friend,' 'The Lady of the Navy' or more commonly and affectionately as simply Aggie.

> Her epitaph reads simply:
>
> ***"The sailor's friend."***

In 1941 during the Second World War, the Rests in both Devonport and Portsmouth were blitzed and destroyed within a few weeks of each other. Some said this was the end of Aggie Weston's, but within a short time canteen work resumed, with a mobile canteen unit provided by the British War Relief Society of the USA. A Few weeks later, a house was rented in Portsmouth and another in Devonport, as temporary accommodation where the Rests were re-established.

As the ways of the Navy changed, the need for accommodation reduced, the charity saw the first Rest to close in Weymouth in

1973. The trustees made the decision for the rests to be known as 'Centres' instead of 'Rests', to resonate with the various sports, activities, events and groups that now took place within them. Some of these included a youth group formed of service children and an Aggie's choir which included staff and beneficiaries.

Even so, due to the dramatic decrease in demand for accommodation with the Navy now providing this facility, the traditional accommodation centres continued to close. The Rowner Centre was the last to close in 2012. Although this is the case, the charity continues to thrive and grow today.

In 2010 the Chaplaincy Support Worker role developed further to Pastoral Workers, the title most of our staff carry today. Aggie's staff now work closely with the RN Chaplaincy in 'Havens' and community teams all over the UK, providing support, and hosting events and activities.

Aggie was a leader, a pioneer of her time, a practical and non-judgmental servant of her beneficiaries and a devout Christian.

She left a comfortable life and selflessly gave all she had for the benefit of others. Her over-riding desire was to offer Christian love to the sailors and their families – because she felt that they needed it.

In her autobiography, she noted that

"My work is, to say the least, varied, and the spirit of love, and I hope common sense, runs through it like a thread of gold."

Aggies legacy was the establishment of a charitable association that continues to work with the same spirit of love for the benefit of the serving members of the Royal Navy and their families to this day.

WHEATLY

Dennis *Wheatly*

Dennis Yeats Wheatley the writer whose prolific output of thrillers and occult novels made him one of the world's best-selling authors from the 1930s through the 1960s.

His Gregory Sallust series was one of the main inspirations for Ian Fleming's James Bond stories.

WHITE

One of my favourite names.

1, Knocker *White*

The most established reason for 'Knocker' is derived from the term used for a Miller's assistant, the 'Knocker'.

The assistant's job was to ensure the mill's hoppers and chutes are kept free from obstructions. This generally ended with the assistant being covered from head to foot in white flour dust.

However, the Knockers job was seasonal. It would last until after the harvest when the last of that year's grain was milled.

To earn enough money to get by many labourers became Marines or Seamen, frequently giving their surname as 'White' in relation to their previous occupation.

2, Chalky *White*

Chalk is white. This version was often foisted on men of African heritage, white being the opposite of black and therefore amusing to Jolly Jack Tar.

3, Nobby *White*

Nobby was a professional boxer who hailed from Canning Town. He was active between 1938 and 1939 and fought at both bantamweight and featherweight.

He took part in 28 professional contests.

4, Isla *White*

A play on words, Isla Wight, a county and the largest and second-most populous island in England.

The island was home to the poets Swinburne and Tennyson and to Queen Victoria, who built her much-loved summer residence and final home, Osborne House, at East Cowes.

6, Snow/Snowy *White.*

From the brother Grimm fairy tale, 'Sneewittchen', first published in 1812. In the 1937 animated film 'Snow White and the Seven Dwarfs' by Walt Disney, the Huntsman is asked by the queen to bring back Snow White's heart and not her lungs and liver as in the original.

WILLIAMS

Bungy *Williams*

The origin of this is disputed. Some say the name is taken from an Australian gangster, others from a singer. But I am going with the following:

Two seamen chippies, Williams and Edwards were given the detail to construct the cask to house Nelson's body until it could be transported back home.

They dutifully did as ordered, but on learning the cask was to be filled with brandy, they added a device for extracting the spirit via the bung.

When the cask eventually arrived in England and was opened to extract Nelson's body, it was found his head was not covered and therefore not pickled as was the rest of his body.

Some say it was evaporation, others that Edwards and Williams received a server flogging. Hence their names shall always be associated with Bungy.

(*Also see 'Edwards'*)

How much of this is true, if any, is rather irrelevant as it would take a rather large black cat to dismiss this dit... But surely this tale is worth a tot to any who might listen in the local tavern one might frequent from time to time?

WILSON/WILLSON

Tug *Wilson*

Derived from the nickname of former First Sea Lord, Admiral of the Fleet Sir Arthur Knyvet Wilson, 3rd Baronet VC, GCB, OM, GCVO was a Royal Navy officer.

Tug served in the Anglo-Egyptian War and the Mahdist War, being awarded the Victoria Cross during the Battle of El Teb in February 1884.

Appointed an advisor at the start of World War I, he advocated offensive schemes in the North Sea, including the capture of Heligoland, and was an early proponent of the development and use of submarines in the Royal Navy.

*The wonderful book **Jackspeak**, tells us this name is after an Admiral Wilson, who upon ordering a battleship to enter harbour and observing the ship's difficulties, offered caustically to its captain to have it towed into port with tugs.*

My research suggests this is the same chap, as he was well known for being "*abrasive, inarticulate and autocratic*", hence the 'short period' he served as First Sea Lord.

WINTERS

Shelly *Winters*

Shelley Winters, actress, won Academy Awards for 'The Diary of Anne Frank' in 1959 and A Patch of Blue in 196).

She received nominations for A Place in the Sun and The Poseidon Adventure.

Her other roles include A Double Life, The Night of the Hunter, Lolita, Alfie and Pete's Dragon.

WITHERS

Googie *Withers*

A cinema and TV actress since the 1930s, Georgette Lizette 'Googie' Withers, a well-known actress during the war and post-war years.

WOOD(S)

1, Timber *Wood*

As in a lumberjack's call.

2, Choppy/Chopper Woods

Simple word association.

3, Slinger *Woods*

Probably a hangover name from the days of the Stevedores who often used slings to move heavy loads on and off ships, including timber planks etc.

WOOLEY

1, Shep *Wooley*

Another word association, Shep or Shepherd being linked to sheep which are (often) woolly.

2, Shep *Wooley*

On the 5th January 1960 Sheb Woolley, (*a nickname borrowed from Shelby Fredrick 'Sheb' Wooley, actor and singer, best known for his 1958 novelty song 'The Purple People Eater. He played Ben Miller, brother of Frank Miller, in the film High Noon; played Travis Cobb in The Outlaw Josey Wales; and was currently starring in TV western series Rawhide*), joined the Navy.

He found many chances to entertain people when off duty and appeared solo or with ships groups all around the world. In the early seventies, he took to stand-up comedy and comedy songwriting and found he had a flair to be able to put over the ordinary matelot's view on service life.

In 1975 Shep, (*he dropped the 'B' in 'sheb' favour of a 'P' as in 'Shep', because it seemed only right someone called Woolley should have a sheep connection*) after a successful appearance on ATV News Faces (*which he did for a bet*), decided to give up his life on board for a life on 'the' boards.

WRIGHT

Shiner *Wright*

Many matelots believe this name came about due to its association with boxing, but the true origin is closer to home.

The name Wright is derived from the Old English 'wyrhta', meaning 'worker', or, specifically, 'woodworker, carpenter, craftsman', and was often used to refer to a ships carpenter.

The 'shiner' in this instant is the hours of polishing and buffing the ships wright undertook to ensure the woodwork, of which there was plenty, was nice and shiny and 'shipshape'.

It simply refers to the laborious task of polishing wood. A bit of a piss-take and typical 'Jack'.

X, Y, & Z

Xray, Yankee & Zulu

YOUNG

1, Brigham *Young*

A religious leader who led Mormon migration to Utah. Brigham Young was an American leader of the Latter-Day Saint movement, politician and a settler in the Western United States.

He was the second president of The Church of Jesus Christ of Latter-day Saints (LDS Church) from 1847 until his death in 1877. He founded Salt Lake City and served as the first governor of the Utah Territory.

2, Jimmy *Young*

Radio one D.J. Sir Leslie Ronald Young CBE, known as Jimmy Young, an English singer, disc jockey and radio personality.

Early in his career, he had two number one records, Unchained Melody and The Man from Laramie, both in 1955, and several other top ten hits, but he became better known for his long-running show on BBC Radio 2.

'Sir Jimmy Young at 90', broadcast on 20 September 2011, heard him in conversation with his friend and former sparring partner Ken Bruce, looking back over his career.

In March 2012 Young returned to presenting on BBC Radio 2 after when he joined Desmond Carrington on a weekly show entitled Icons of the '50s.

Odds & Sods

Although most Navy nicknames are based on people's surnames, others are given according to a person's physical appearance or a personality trait and occasionally their job/branch/rank.

Jack, in his wisdom, often, or should I say frequently, picks the form of nickname based on a person's most unsympathetic personal features and qualities.

It is possible in this cotton wool, manby pamby modern world, some bleeding heart or artist may interpret this as a form of bullying, but they miss the entire point by a nautical mile.

No nickname, however harsh it may seem to anyone who has not served in front of a grey funnel, is anything but inclusive. Nicknames are, by their very nature, character building and a badge of acceptance to be worn and bragged about with pride.

These are some of the more common. (The boring ones):

Blue   A red-headed person

Bones A very slim - even skinny person "all skin & bones" or a sickbay tiffy, doc or nurse.

Curly   A curly-headed person. Also, on the negative, a straight-haired or bald person

Dutch(y) Anyone of Dutch extraction or any Dutch name

Eggy Usually a someone overweight, and predominantly a short person.

Lofty A tall person, or someone very short.

Paddy an Irishman.

Scottie a Scotsman.

Shorty A short person, or a very tall person.

Slim or **Splinter** A slim and/or tall person.

The following are some of the more unusual and fun names.

These were forwarded to me for inclusion in The Andrew, Jack & Jenny.

These are listed in the order received.

JUMPFER, given to a rating with the surname Joy.

NIPPLE, *because he was a 'tit'.* This name was bestowed on the lucky recipient at Fisgard.

Circa 1906's:

A 'coloured guy', (*nowadays read 'a person of African descent'*), held the surname of Valmar. **Val** for short.

This dear man was therefore christened with the nickname of '**VAL COONICAN**', (*a pisstake of Val Doonican, an Irish singer of traditional pop, easy listening, and novelty songs popular in the 1950's to early 1980's).*

Clearly, this is not a 'PC' name and would not now be considered acceptable.

Then there was **STICKY PAIGE**. It seems he had to explain this name to his (*newlywed*) wife.

Oh, and *Kerr* was known as **WAYNE.**

One name given because of a personality trait was **THROMBO**, "B*ecause he was a slow-moving clot.*"

Another was **COT DEATH** given for his amazing ability to sleep. *(I am uncertain how this may be received nowadays?)*

It is also known two excellent leading hands, both of Rhodesian birth, held the names of '**OMO**' & '**DAZ**' respectively. *(Non-pc I guess.)*

One of my favourites was '**ENA**' after the Coronation Street character *Ena Sharples*.

A relatively unliked crab fat pilot called Ball was known below decks as '**ORI**', so his full name became '**Oriball**'.

The TV show 'Roots' was responsible for a young skin by the name of '*Kinder*' to become known as '**KUNTA**'. The supplier of this information said 'Kunta Kinta' was '*A bit harsh but as funny as fuck.*'

In the 1990's, serving on a T22 were two oppos, one called *Mapp* the other *Dye*. They were known as **TREASURE & PRINCESS**.

STREEKA was a tall skinny lad. (*streak of piss*)

Anyone who knew a seaman called *Smallbone* would know him better by the name of '**CHOPPER**'.

PLANK was given to a rather 'slow to catch on' seaman.

HEALTHY was fitting for someone called '*Feltwell*' (*Cherry B*).

A Fist Aid Nursing Yeoman (*City of London*) called *Cummings* became known as **FANNY**.

There was, of course, a chap whose name was *P. Harder.*

I like that *Nixon Eckersall* was bestowed the mantle of **NIX & SOX**.

Then a junior cook named *Issitt...* also known as **ORNOT.**

It is said a draft was swapped with someone called *R. O. Tate*.

I'll leave you with the self-introduction line said by a pilot from the Iron Duke with the name of *Richard Pounder*.

"Hello, I'm Dick Pounder".

There are, I know, many more earned/given names of individual excellence which merit mentioning as Jack was forever inventive, but it would take an entire series of books to list them all, so the above samples are all I am adding to *this edition* of The Andrew, Jack & Jenny.

Jenny's Nicknames

This is the most disappointing section of this book with regards to the number of names I have been able to confirm and authenticate.

It seems Jennies did not share the same affinity with nicknames as the rest of the navy.

During my research for this book, most of the nicknames relating to Jennies are the derogatory ones given by matelots.

Such basic and known generics such as *Splits*, *Split Arses* or *Lumpy Jumpers*, who all lived in the Wrens quarters known as the *Mattress store*.

Which is a shame, knowing the high esteem in which Jennies are held.

However, this book would not be complete without me giving some examples, so here are the few nicknames I have been supplied by those kind enough to send them to me.

A wren in 771 Squadron whose was called *Goodhead* became known as **BJ.**

A (*nameless*) wren in Mersey Division RNR was known as **YOYO KNICKERS.**

Illustrious was home to **K5** (*the name given to a spare boiler*).

Another whose surname was *Hindley*, so it is with little surprise she became known as **MYRA.**

A *K**** Burges* was bestowed the name of **TIMBERWOLF.** (*I'll let you dwell on that one.*)

"We had one (*Jenny*) at Whitehall Comcen who was known as the **SILVERBACK** 'cos when she came in the office it was like a scene out of Gorillas in the Mist."

"When at Sultan in '78 doing AMC, one of the Jenny's had a half-set. She was called **CHEWBACCA** after the big hairy f***er on Star Wars."

"I was once told by an old Chief, Jennies were briefly called *Turtles*. Because once they are on their backs they are f****d. By all accounts, this '*nickname*' was stamped out very quickly. I can't think why."

"The Endurance had a wren Fleet Joss named **SUE THE CHEW**, I gather she liked FAA fleet gun crews."

"I remember one I served with a couple of times, name *C***/ Ledwidge*, nickname **LULU**, because of her likeness to the singer of that era."

"*Howard* in my baby wrens class back in '71 was named **FRANKIE**."

"**DIZZY LIZZIE** was in Portsmouth around 1972."

"**PORTHLEVEN JANE**, not that I ever knew the lady, in a biblical sense or any other sense, you understand?"

(*Me thinkith the man protesteth too much!*)

"There was a Wren at Whitehall in '80-81 who wore huge 'Deirdre Barlow' glasses, nicknamed **OLLIE**."

A Scottish Jenny at Culdrose was known as **DIRTY DOTTY** *with a spotty botty*. She could drink most matelots under the table.

Oh, and there was **ET** at Sultan.

"Unfortunately for her, there was a wren whose actual name was *Cocks*. She was always known as **SUCKS**".

"There was a girl on Intrepid who apparently looked like Michael Jackson's chimp and got "**BUBBLES**" … until she started packing some weight on, then she got, "**FULL STOP**". (*little, black and round*).

"I recall **BENDY WENDY** on the Ark."

"The Jenny who dished out the rum in Dolphin in '65 was called **NELLY NO NECK**."

"I remember the names of two wrens in Vernon, **SWAN VESTA** was tall thin with red hair, the other **WAN EATA** had only a single front tooth."

(*This was in the '50/60).*

THIRSTY KIRSTIE was on the Ark in 2003.

"Her Surname was *Ruff* and the ship she served on was the *Beaver?*"

(I am unsure how true this one is.)

"I remember a couple of girls called **HINGE & BRACKET** in Northwood around 1980. Not called that to their faces but universally known as such as they hung around together almost 24/7."

(Named after a female comedy duo of the time.)

A PO WREN at Northwood who worked either in the fleet commcen or NILU.... they used to call her "**ROPEY ROPKEY.**"

"When I was at Mercs in the 70's there was a Wren with the surname *Zelmutt*, we used to call her **BOBBY.**"

(Say it over a few times and you'll get it.)

Another called *Bramble* ended up being '**PRICKLY**'.

There was also **SEXY EXLEY,** who became **SPEXLEY** when she started wearing glasses.

Not forgetting G**l *Marshall*. Known to all as **TEX.**

Some other Jennies names, given without explanation are:

Head & Shoulders

Snooker table

Train smash

Violent Vera

Masie Fat Paps

Liver Lips Louise

Sweaty Sandra

That's all I have for now.

If you served in the WRNS and would like to inform me of genuine nicknames given to you or your colleagues, I will keep records and I shall add them when I revised and updated The Andrew, Jack & Jenny.

Email me at pwauthor@mail.com

Afterword

Thank you for reading The Andrew, Jack & Jenny.

I learnt much I did not know during my research into Royal Navy nicknames. I found many of the facts I uncovered fascinating, others wonderous and some simply beguiling.

Whether the origin or the history surrounding our names are believable or unbelievable, reading The Andrew, Jack & Jenny can stir memories of long-forgotten shipmates, places we visited and adventures played out on beaches, in the back streets and within hidden bars; the often dingy watering holes which, it seemed were known only by Jack.

Most of those places and memories we hold dear have vanished or altered so much they are no longer the places we knew, the ones where we went ashore for a postcard or a rabbit run, the DTS's and raucous nights ashore; when we staggered back to our ship, grabbing some big eats on the way.

Those places have long gone, buried under steel and concrete, now sporting shiny new burgers bars and coffee shops, but our names, our Naval nicknames remain unchanged, they are a permeant reminder of those times, the places, the people, the shore bases, our ships, the far-flung cities and beaches, the harbours and ports strung around the globe, each and every one a playground for Jack.

A playground where our Royal Navy nicknames were spoken aloud, places where our names shall echo forevermore.

About the Author

Paul White is a prolific storyteller, a wordsmith, tale weaver and an Amazon international bestselling author.

He writes from his Yorkshire home, situated near a quiet market town in the East Ridings.

Paul has published several books, from full-length novels to short story collections, poetry, children's books, semi-fiction and military social history.

He is also a contributor to various collective anthologies.

You can find out more about Paul, his current works-in-progress, artworks, photography and other projects, by visiting his website:

http://paulznewpostbox.wix.com/paul-white

OTHER BOOKS BY PAUL WHITE

Fiction

The Abduction of Rupert DeVille

(Paperback & eBook)

Tales of Crime & Violence

(Volumes 1, 2 & 3)

Dark Words

Dark Tales – Darker poetry

(Paperback)

Within the Invisible Pentacle

(Paperback)

Semi-Fiction

Life in the War Zone

(Paperback)

Poetry

Teardrops & White Doves

(Paperback, eBook & Outsized Hardcover)

THE ANDREW, JACK & JENNY

Shadows of Emotion

(Paperback & eBook)

Military Social History

HMS Tiger -Chronicles of the last big cat

(Outsized Hardcover only)

The Pussers Cook Book

(Paperback & Hardcover)

Jack's Dits

(Paperback)

Children's stories

The Rabbit Joke

(Outsized Hardcover)

Music /Art

Iconic

(Hardcover only)

PAUL WHITE

Anthologies

(Joint Author/contributor)

Awethors anthology – Light volume

Awethors December anthology – Dark volume

Individually Together

(Storybook publishing)

Violence, Control & other kinds of Love

(Abyssinian press)

Looking into the Abyss

(TOAD Publishing)

A Treasure chest of children's stories

(Plaisted publishing house)

Midsummer Anthology

(Jara publishing)